Hamlyn

London New York Sydney Toronto

Editor and Designer
GAVIN PETRIE

Published by the Hamlyn Publishing Group Limited
London · New York · Sydney · Toronto
Astronaut House, Feltham, Middlesex, England
in association with IPC Specialist and Professional Press



ISBN 0600313433

Printed in West Germany by Mohn-Gordon Ltd.

James Brown . . . . . . . . . . 4
Ray Charles . . . . . . . . . . . 11
Staple Singers . . . . . . . . . . 16
O'Jays . . . . . . . . . . . . . . . 27
3 Degrees . . . . . . . . . . . . . 32
Chi Lites . . . . . . . . . . . . . 38
Thom Bell . . . . . . . . . . . . 41
Bill Withers . . . . . . . . . . . 45
Pointer Sisters . . . . . . . . . . 54
Barry White . . . . . . . . . . . 59
Maytals . . . . . . . . . . . . . . 64
John Holt . . . . . . . . . . . . . 71
Isley Brothers . . . . . . . . . 76
Harold Melvin . . . . . . . . 82
Smokey Robinson . . . . . . 91
Stylistics . . . . . . . . . . . . . 96
War . . . . . . . . . . . . . . . . . 103
Al Green . . . . . . . . . . . . . 108
Bobby Bland . . . . . . . . . . 115
Dandy Livingstone . . . . . . 119
Billy Preston . . . . . . . . . . 124

# James Brown

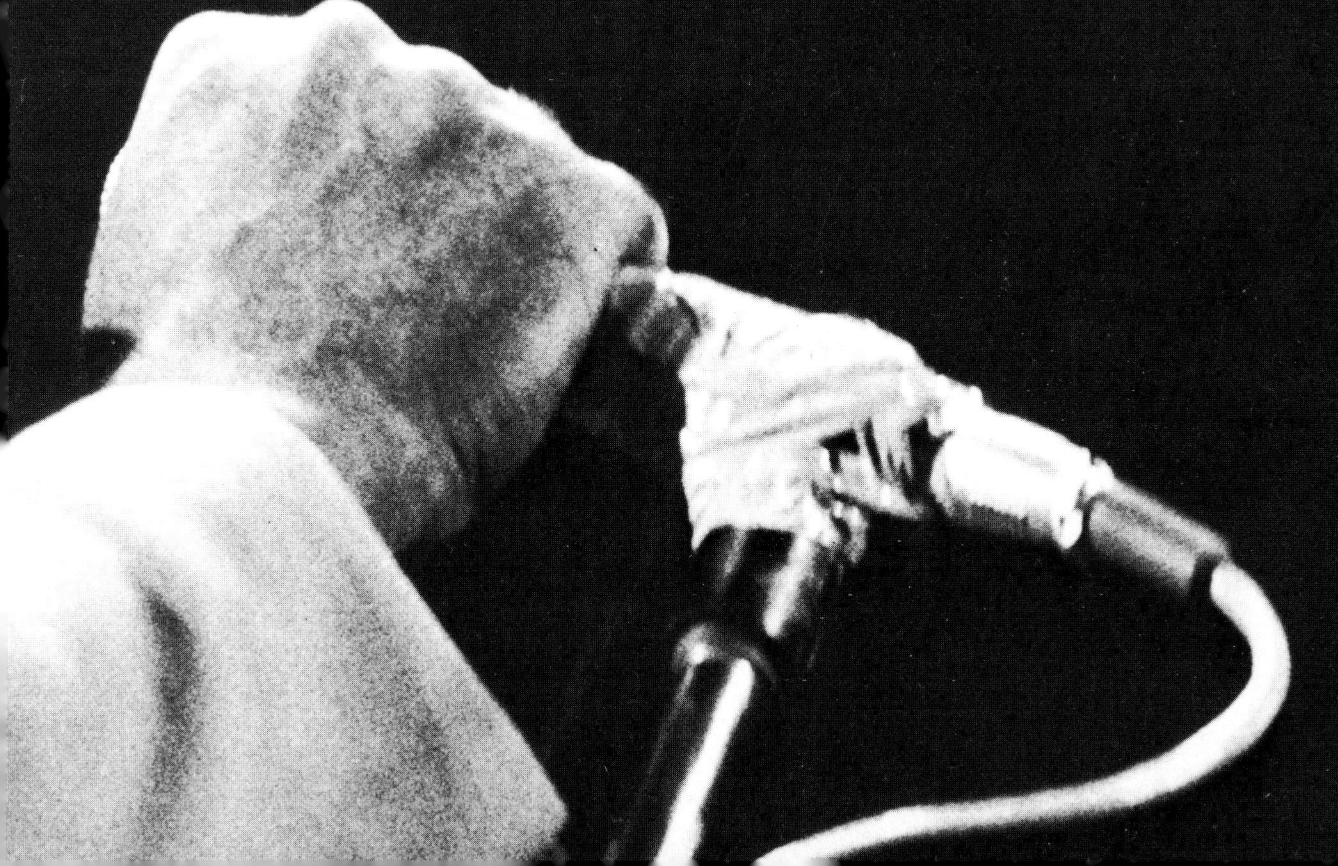

**OF all the flamboyant personalities, sex idols, dynamic performers and plain old superstars, James Brown outbids them all. Louder, longer, and harder.**

And why? Because he *is* what you see. There's no shy pretender behind the image; he believes every word, he lives every action, his own personality is the source of every peak in his career. The essence of his story is not so much the rungs of his ladder to success, but the determination with which he fought his way to the top, and the energy which keeps him sitting there still. This character today, at over 40, is cutting records with more drive, more *guts*, than young studs half his age.

A volatile mixture of pride, anger, and ambition, hardened by an astute instinct for survival. A man who just had to prove himself and got so wrapped up in the heat of the fight and the uncertainty of success that he's never found the security to slacken his pace nor lower his guard. To be part of James Brown's vision is to be on the case. A world peopled by heroes and villians, where the women are proud and hot-pant sexy, and the men love hard, fight tough, and live life to its limits. It could be a fantasy, except there he is, larger than life, to back up every gesture. For James Brown is not composing songs about some make-believe existence, he *is* his music. Soul at its roots. Partying to a James Brown record is to tap a source of energy where anything is possible. The invitation is open to anyone who cares to listen.

When James Brown screams, "you got to use what you got to get just what you want" he's being as true to himself as John Lee Hooker mumbling "Stuttering Blues" or Ray Charles drowning in his own tears. It's just that before Mr. Dynamite the world had not experienced anyone with quite so much fire in his belly. With few exceptions, the very best records of James Brown have been his own compositions, cut with his own band. Not even songs in the accepted sense, but pure expressions of potency, sensuality and power. Pulses of energy that crackle off the vinyl like whip lashes. There have been some masterly slow performances too. Not ballads though, more like dirges. For he's a man of extremes. When James Brown is down he's not vaguely maudlin, he's shattered, *distraught*, screaming and hollering till there's nowhere to go but up.

The most immediate tap to the power line is the stage show and still there is nothing comparable. To see The James Brown Revue today is to experience two hours of skilfully judged orgasms of the senses. From the stimulating funk of The J.B.'s, through the persuasive caresses of Lyn Collins, to climax in a second-half of frenetic total commitment as Brown picks up his audience and carries the whole theatre on a trip through degrees of eroticism and challenge guaranteed to wring emotion out of the dullest body.

Listen to the message . . . Get On The Good Foot baby, 'cause I Got Ants In My Pants. Let's give it some Soul Power, Hot Pants, you know I'm Superbad. So Try Me, and Make It Funky. C'mon Sex Machine—I Got A Bag Of My Own. Dowee, Stoned To The Bone! A message delivered in a non-stop whirl of sound, lights and movement as Brown spins, strides, splits, jerks and shimmies in a sea of irridescent strobes. His legs and feet are never still, pumping and shuffling to the rhythm; his hips have a life of their own, grinding to the beat; his arms weave a pattern of beating wings about him, first on his hips, then over his shoulder, then signalling to the band, now whipping back to hurl the mike stand out over the audience and back again as he falls with it to the crack of a rim-shot and a synchronized twirl from the brass section. His head thrown back in a scream of agony and triumph, a distorted mask framed in a tangle of deranged black hair. It is a masterpiece of theatre.

And yet the show is a mere half the size it was, and there are obvious signs that each year sees a little less gymnastics thrown into the arena. Can you imagine what it was like 8–10 years ago? When the band was 20 strong and there were four warm-up soloists, two vocal groups, a comedian and a troupe of dancers. And when Brown was the fittest thing on two legs outside of the Olympics. It's unlikely that there'll ever be anything quite like it again, except his own continual evolvement and the shadows of the phenomenon that can be seen in every road show from Sly to The Rolling Stones. Ike Turner, for one, must have bought a monthly season ticket for front row seats, so closely does his own show try to follow Brown's.

Histories of superstars have a way of falling into a pattern: lean years-hustling years-limited recognition-breakthrough-glory. Brown's has been traced so often the facts fall with the dull thud of a publicity handout. The barefoot country kid picking up coals from railroad tracks; adolescent outcast in the ghetto, shining shoes and calling reform school home; the struggling vocal trio; the first regional hit and the gigs around the cheap dance halls of the south; the first national hit. You can see the pattern building. But whereas the pace of other artist's careers has depended on how the luck of events has led them through these stages, Brown systematically reversed the flow of influence. He was the first black entertainer to gain such complete control over his own destiny. To appreciate the scale of this achievement is to realise just how fundamental he has been to the major upheaval that has brought black musicians out from under the yoke of white control. And to see this is to begin to understand his music.

The spark that ignited the flame that caused the explosion was "Try Me." Recorded in September 1958 it was Brown's first national hit, struggling to the dizzy height of 48 on Billboard's Hot 100 in November of that year. It's probably the nearest he has come to beauty in his entire recorded output. A slow, gospelly plea—Darling, tell me "I need you"—delivered with uncharacteristic tenderness, that introduced him (with The Famous Flames) to a new public across the States. Then, The Flames were as close to Brown as rhythm is to blues. It is no surprise that they were relentlessly eclipsed as their driving force broke out of the bonds of their relationship. For, as the longest serving Flame, Bobby Byrd, admitted: "I gotta face the truth. Without James we were just another group. I mean, we were all important but he was the star." The name on the record label merely fell in line with the reality of the content—James Brown. He had the vision, the others were only there for the ride.

Apart from "Please Please Please" (the first issue—the song that captured the record contract in Feb '56) few of the ten releases before "Try Me" stirred any interest outside of Georgia and the Carolinas, and even there they were no big thing as yet. Already though, Brown was their undisputed leader. He was the only Flame that turned up at every gig, he was the only voice to be heard on all tracks from every session, *and* he was writing most of the group's material. But he was still writing for a group. The songs had not yet acquired the clear individuality of their creator. They were mainly uninspired derivations, drawn from his gospel experience and the popular acts about him. A pastiche of The Midnighters, The Five Royals and Charles Brown with a dash of Little Richard.

"Try Me" changed everything. With a national hit under his belt he got himself a contract with booking agent Ben Bart at Universal Attractions; a road band, the J. C. Davis outfit; and a whole new set of ideas. Being able to rely on a well-rehearsed band who knew their man had a telling effect on his writing. Using them to punctuate and emphasise the vocal interplay between himself and The Flames he created a more exact reflection of his ego, and notched up twelve hits in a row. By 1960 the Northern states were getting to

know the man who was now cleaning up down South. "Good Good Lovin'"—"I'll Go Crazy"—"This Old Heart"—"Think"—"You've Got The Power"—"The Bells"—"Bewildered"—"I Don't Mind"—"I'll Never Never Let You Go"—"Lost Someone"—"Night Train"—"Shout And Shimmy"—set new standards in excitement, introducing to black America the raw bones of a sound that was to help mould the structure of its music through to the present day.

As the music became an expression of his inner drive, so did the stage show expand to the limits of his imagination. It must be remembered that these were not the easy days of short star concerts where half-a-dozen choruses and a curtain call are the rule of thumb. He was appearing in dance halls and empty arenas where the entrance fee guaranteed a full evenings entertainment—and James Brown was determined to be *the* biggest name around. He took every known routine in the book, honed them to a keen perfection, and then threw in just as many of his own. His hair styles became the wildest, his clothes the slickest, and those dances . . . The fastest and most energetic ever seen. Off stage he was developing talents that would take him higher than any black entertainer had ever achieved independent of white manipulation. He was learning the business. Setting the charges to break down barriers that, once blown, made it easier for everyone who followed in his wake.

He started his lessons back in '56 when he was a know-nothing country boy relying on Syd Nathan, president of his record company King, to give him an even deal. "In those days there was a little grocery store in front of King's building where everybody would hang out, drinking beer and wine, and rapping. All the cats on the label hung in there. Billy Ward, Hank Ballard, Otis Williams, everybody. With the store so close to the studio there was always cases of booze at the sessions. We took it for granted, figuring it for a groovy deal. When it was time for our first royalty statement Mr. Nathan had charged us for everything. Travel expenses from Georgia, rent in Cincinatti, studio costs, tape costs, musicians, just everything. At the bottom of the list was over $100 for miscellaneous expenses. It turned out those expenses were for every bottle of beer we had used up in the studio. We were all mad because we figured we had some big money coming from 'Please'. After the deductions there wasn't much to collect."

He didn't get caught again. Immediately he started taking an intense interest in contracts. When he signed to Universal Attractions he dropped his first manager, Cint Brantley, and latched onto Ben Bart, who was only too willing to concentrate on such obvious potential. Soon he was getting a percentage of the gate as well as his performing fee, then he got in on the promoters cut, then they were partners, then he was making all the decisions, and finally in the late '60s he dropped Bart and was running the whole shooting match himself.

Of course it wasn't as simple as that. Back in 1958 he was still very much under the wing of Syd Nathan, and it took those years of solid hits for the old man to be convinced that Brown knew what he was doing. As the road show expanded and gained in popularity, Brown was eager to get the band on record. Side-stepping Nathan's reluctance he went to Henry Stone in Miami and had them recorded as Nat Kendrick and The Swans (Kendrick was then the drummer). "Mashed Potatoes", a dance routine that was causing riots on stage, was an instrumental hit in 1960. Won over by this demonstration Nathan then agreed to record the band for King ("Hold It" etc). This reversal illustrates the kind of insistence Brown brought to bear on his whole career.

If 1958–62 were the years when the stage show and each record became a true reflection of Brown's character, it was 1963–4 that unleashed the full power of the man across the U.S.A. On October 24, 1962 a live recording was made of the show at the famed Apollo Theatre, New York. It's impossible to overestimate the impact of this record. R & B radio stations played it like a single, devoting periods to the entire L.P. For the first time blacks en masse bought an album, and whites began to get an inkling of this amazing performer, hitherto unknown outside of the ghetto. In 1963 Brown was voted No. 1 R & B singer of America—he was on his way.

It became increasingly obvious to Brown that King records were just not geared to keep pace with his rapidly expanding horizons. Although Nathan was by now a firm believer in Brown's talent (and becoming ever dependent on him to bring in the label's profits) his ideas were rooted in the fifties and the whole set up was gradually slipping behind the more dynamic companies in the industry. Nathan's approach was to persuade Brown to record four syrupy ballads in front of a large orchestra with string section and a heavenly choir. The traditional gambit of making overtures to the supper-club/concert hall circuit. The same policy that castrated Ray Charles and threw Motown fans into confusion a few years later. It must be admitted there that "Prisoner Of Love", from this session, became one of Brown's great performances, but only because he changed the structure of the whole song. On stage it was delivered like a 20-minute sermon from the wailingest of store-front preachers. *Not* the kind of thing to wow them at The Copacabana.

Brown and Bart were sharper. Together they formed Fair Deal Productions and delivered the next batch of tapes to Smash Records of Chicago, a division of the nationwide Mercury Corp. Among the tracks was "Out Of Sight". The first of his records to sell in large quantities to whites (because of Smash's blanket coverage), it heralded a new era of Brown's music as he shrugged off the remaining clouds of King's outdated atmosphere. He had invaded a lucrative new market while retaining his artistic integrity. If anything, the records became even more just an extension of the man. He phased out The Flames and brought up the band, emphasising the strong rhythm accompaniment. The songs, at that time still set in a recognizable framework, gradually became less formally constructed. By the end of the sixties many were little more than thoughts and emotions spat out over a complex series of shifting rhythms. As he so clearly defined it a year after the change, "Papa's Got A Brand New Bag". The bag was a sense of unrestrained confidence that comes only with success and the sure fire knowledge of achievement. He was a generation ahead of his time. Only with the more favourable climate in the aftermath of Brown's breakthrough have black personalities emerged from years of subordinate influence to parallel his independence—and their music become more aggressively personalised.

When King's lawyers forced an injunction against Smash, restricting them to issuing only instrumentals under J. B.'s name and those records made by the artists in the revue, Brown stubbornly refused to go back to his former company. For nearly a year there was

Brown
flashbacks . . .

a stand-off while Nathan grew ever more desperate to get his major artist back, and Brown had to rely on King's reissues to keep his name in the charts. Nathan broke first, and offered him the works. Brown returned to King with all the reins at his command, giving them "Papa's Bag". He now had complete control over all aspects of his recording career; the road show, under director Nat Jones, was at its largest; and, thanks to his flirtation with Smash, both blacks and whites were boosting each new release high into the charts.

In 18 years and well over 100 releases Brown has never hit the No. 1 spot in the Hot 100, and a mere six of his records have made the top ten. Cold statistics that only go to prove the chart is no barometer of popularity, nor an arbiter of good taste. What it does highlight is the influence of the media's fickle interest. For most of his career Brown has been treated indifferently by press and TV alike, but for the four years following his dramatic arrival in whitey's life he was bathed in a fashionable spotlight. Nationwide TV programmes were glad to book him; teen mags treated him like a pimply pop star; and even on this side of The Atlantic dear old Ready, Steady, Go gave him an entire show (to the outrage of thousands). It was this period that carried his half-dozen toptenners: "Papa's Got A Brand New Bag" (September '65)—"I Got You" (December '65)—"It's A Man's World" (June '66)—"Cold Sweat" (September '67)—"I Got The Feelin'" (May '68)—"Say It Loud, I'm Black And I'm Proud" (October '68).

This last title, the spontaneous anthem born of the street riots that summer, climaxed the most confusing year of Brown's career. He'd started in January by buying the first of his radio stations; in the Spring he flew to the Ivory Coast, at the request of their government; later to Vietnam for Uncle Sam; and following his dramatic TV appearances after the assassination of Dr. Martin Luther King he was dragged headlong into the political arena. For the first time he was possibly out of his depth. Feted by white politicians and harangued by black militants he was on the rollercoaster to chaos. But the charges of 'Tom-ism" were ill-founded, for a U.S. writer Alan Leeds observed: "Brown has always welcomed acceptance among whites, but never bargains for it at the expense of his roots." That was never more true than of his reaction to 1968. From out of the turmoil came a new, stronger conviction. A reaffirmed commitment that drove his music with urgent exhilaration—straight into the seventies.

In battling his way to the top Brown forged about himself a shield of ruthless steel to brush aside scorn, prejudice, and any would-be competitors. As a result, bitter remarks and unsavoury rumours have churned in his wake for years. On examination, most of these allegations can be seen as pure jealousy, but there are undoubtedly deep-rooted reactions in the man that set him apart from contemporaries. Anyone else would have long past the point where they needed to prove themselves to the world, yet he has never allowed himself the good-humoured civility of others who took their chances at a more leisurely pace. As Jerry Butler confessed to Alan Leeds: "I feel helpless around him. I wanna love this man as a brother so badly but he makes it damm near impossible. I love his music, it's so real, but I just try to stay away from him. I know that if we're together he'll say something demeaning or unnecessary to make me mad. It's insane for a man of his talent to lower himself to that line of bullshit."

Public slanging matches with challengers like Joe Tex and Wilson Pickett dog his career; the claustrophobic atmosphere of his autocratic empire has led to a constant flow of personnel, particularly band members seekking greater artistic liberty; and a blind insistence in his own judgment has produced some horrendous lapses of taste on his records. And yet, without the years of blinkered perseverance the James Brown legend would not exist; with each change the band grows tighter, moving along with the tide of time; and it is precisely the unwavering egocentricity of the man that gives his music its unique flavour. If there are flaws, who's the loser? Perhaps only Brown himself, bound to the isolation of self-styled omnipotence.

It's certainly not his public, for on stage and on record James Brown is patently, almost overwhelmingly, sincere. The show is rehearsed to the nth degree and set in a showcase of pure theatre, but it is still 100 per cent of the man. On disc, the mediocre tracks fade into obscurity beneath the endless stream of releases that he floods onto the market.

That river of emotion has never been stronger than over the last six years; arguably the most exciting, and consistent, period of his entire career. Just check the titles. The last with his famous sixties band; "Give It Up Or Turnit A Loose"—"I Don't Want Nobody To Give Me Nothin'"—"Mother Popcorn"—"Let A Man Come In"—"It's A New Day." The first with the new, younger, group, as he wound up his association with King: "Sex Machine"—"Superbad"—"Talkin' Loud And Sayin' Nothing" (withheld for two years)—"Get Up, Get Into It, And Get *Involved*"—"Soul Power"—"Hot Pants." And recently, the tracks cut with his tightest, and most popular, group, The J.B.s. An amalgam of old friends and new faces, fused together to testify to Brown's enduring ability to package his emotions in a contemporary framework. Now internationally distributed through the Polydor complex: "Make It Funky"—"I'm A Greedy Man"—"There It Is"—"Get On The Good Foot" etc—maintain a pitch of involvement that other artists are proud to achieve, perhaps, once or twice in a lifetime.

Because Brown's music has remained so intensely personal he has consistently provoked the most extreme opinions from critics and the public alike. Vitriolic attacks and reverent adulation go hand-in-hand with each new James Brown record. Which side of the fence you stand depends entirely on whether his pulse triggers your circuit; but opinion aside, straight facts stand as a monument to his contribution to black music. His message is encouragement through example. The hard fought trail from the dirt of South Carolina to a mogul's hot-seat is the plot of the story; over 80 national chart entries, even more in the R&B lists, fill in the detail of the chapters; and the individuality of his music infuses the whole with vivid, if somewhat biased, confidence. You don't need to enjoy the vocabulary to appreciate the scope of the drama.

In 1974 Brown displays as much restless vitality as he did nearly 20 years ago. A propelling urge that will be the heart-beat of black music until the day this major power source shuts down, when, like the stilled turbines of some vast liner, he collapses and dies on stage. By now, enough other artists have picked up his momentum to prevent the whole movement drifting back onto stony ground, but while he lives, James Brown is not the man to let them outrun him. His latest surge of funk, "The Payback", is the grittiest mutha he's ever let loose. Seven minutes of devastating put-down that throbs with the pain of a lifetime's fight. The album around it indicates, yet again, that subtle changes of approach are on the way; a forewarning of another twenty years reign for The Godfather Of Soul—James Brown.

# Ray Charles

**JUST in case it's a legend you never learnt: Born Ray Charles Robinson, Albany, Georgia, September 23, 1932 . . . blind since the age of six . . . orphaned at 15 . . . greatest early influences Nat 'King' Cole and Charles Brown . . . formed own band Maxim Trio at 17 . . . worked around Seattle . . . recorded L.A., 1948, Swingtime Records . . . regional success . . . moved to Atlantic 1952 . . . massive hits . . . became huge star . . . success, concerts, hit records.**

Writing a short feature on Ray Charles is like writing in 500 words the complete history of the world. Everyone does—or should—know that Ray is the father of soul, a living legend, the first soul brother, a genius. So who needs an endless list of million selling records, descriptions of sell-out Carnegie Hall concerts, academic analyses of Ray's technique of fusing a gospel music style into jazz, blues and pop or earnest eulogies about the effect of Ray's heart-tearing vocals?

One major thing should be said, though. Over the last decade something *sad* has happened to Uncle Ray. Not to his finances. You can't harm a legend who can pull down a million bucks a year in concert fees alone and who doesn't need million sellers or even hit records to retain superstar status. What's saddening is Ray's realisation of the fact. For a good few years the singles and albums ABC have poured into the market have been Ray performing either bland, mechanical attempts to revive the power of "I Gotta Woman" or the poignancy of "You Don't Know Me", or alternatively clumsy efforts to update his churchy, soul-jazz-blues style into the new super-soul groove—and in the process merely adopting the cliches, and not the spirit, of the newer black music.

But possibly the saddest thing of all has been the passé image of yesterday's hero

which the young black music followers have saddled him with. In a way, who can blame them? What relevance in this age of "What's Going On", Sly Stone, the Philly Sound and street funk, has this tuxedo-and-bow-tied singer/pianist, singing the hits of Irving Berlin on Streisand TV specials?

That isn't easy to answer. Ray's never going to give to us again that same thrill of discovery, that "What'd I Say" did in 1959 or "Hit The Road Jack" in 1961. Nor, for that matter, now that producers have figured out how to effectively use strings behind R&B artists, is the charm of "Take These Chains From My Heart" going to again quite make up for its cloying sentimentality.

How Ray *is* relevant is that black music isn't, or shouldn't be about the flimsy ephemera of pop star 'images'. It doesn't matter what the guy looks like, how old he is, his taste in clothes or how happily he fits into the showbiz, Vegas nitery, concerts-at-the-White-house world.

A lot of record reviewers over the last few years have pointed out the cliched but true fact that many of the ABC discs have been as drab as a wet Monday. But what is also true is that a few of Uncle Ray's later ABC sides (try "Your Turn To Cry" or "Your Love Is So Doggone Good") have all the magic of the old Ray. Inspiration over the last few years may have shown through in increasingly meagre spurts but when Ray's good, he's *good*.

In late 1973, after more than a decade with ABC, Ray left and with his manager formed his own record company. He'd done something similar before of course: for years he'd run the successful Tangerine outfit. But now he was breaking clear of huge corporations. Crossover Records has so far had more impact for Ray with one single and one album than five times that amount of ABC product. Why? Another tough question. His U.S. hit single "Come Live With Me" is another of those country-weepies-with-strings that he's re-

verted to at regular intervals since '62 when "Modern Sounds In Country & Western Music" topped the album charts.

There's nothing "new" in "Live". So why the hit? And why did BM editor Alan Lewis applaud in such rapturous terms one side of the "Come Live With Me" Album released here on London ("side two is true grit: all snorting horns, smouldering electric piano and churchy shouts from the Raelets, with Ray grooving out on some strong, soulful songs"). Because folks, when Ray's good, he's *good.* Ray says it a bit differently. Ray says a lot of things a bit differently.

"People sometimes ask me if I'm happy with *all* the records I've made . . . hell, that's some damn question. I'm happy with *some* of the records I've made. I guess those where I'm into a more relaxed thing, closer to my roots. The roots of my music is what I honestly feel. Now if that happens to carry the label of R&B then I'll accept it, though I don't care what label they give it. I just sing exactly what I feel . . . period. Some people say my style comes from the church-singing in gospel choirs, and some people say it's jazz, but really my music comes from what I'm doing at home. I just sing about *life* you know.

"There is nothing specific that I feel I still want to record. Things just come together when time comes for a new session. Mind, I first get the ideas what I want to do, I don't just walk into the studio and record *anything.* I record strictly to a set plan. On the 'Come Live With Me' album I do some ballad things, the kinda stuff that goes down well with older audiences you know like 'Till There Was You' and 'If You Go Away'. Sid Feller did the string arrangements. But I do some funky ol' things too you know (the brilliant 'Somebody' and a charming piece of tempo-changing poignancy 'Everybody Sing') I feel some of those are some of the best things I've cut. I'm excited with Crossover, I'm gonna stretch it out and I hope to build it into a *big, big* company.

"I'm not just relying on myself as an artist. I'm producing other artists. I'm working with a lady who plays real, real great piano and also sings very well. Her name is Clydine Jackson. We are also working with the Edwards Brothers, not only are they both singers and musicians but they write songs themselves. Rather like Stevie Wonder. Also we have the Simms Twins—yeah, the guys who made 'Soothe Me'. And naturally there is always the Raelets.

"We want to do a well rounded thing, so that artists can come in and sing and play songs that can go into another field. In other words "crossover", like our name says. We're gonna get entertainers who are capable of covering both sides of the music thing, black and white. Rather like myself you know. You know if they want to go in and jam some jazz they can do that, if they want to do rhythm and blues they can do that.

"For my own records, I'm working on a new LP now. Billy Preston and I were supposed to go in the studios. We wanted to record something together. The two of us wanted to do it but we couldn't, because of our different contracts. That was really sad because both of us have worked together over the years. Of course I helped give Billy his start in the business. I've followed Billy's career. I'm very proud of what he has done now.

"You know, this new enterprise has given me a fresh taste for recording. I feel kinda excited about the projects I'm working on. I think I need to spend a bit longer on my records than I might have done in the past, so I get the kinda groove going that really pleases me. Because of Crossover, I'm cutting down on the number of shows I'm doing. I do about five months out of a year.

"We hope to be back in England soon. You see we always come to Europe each fall like October and I had this idea—I don't know how good it is—to play in the Spring as a change. And that's not the only thing that's changing for me."

# Staple Singers

**IT isn't hard to imagine a concert hall staging an "Authentic Blues Festival". Paul Oliver would make the introduction for the adoring crowd of earnest young men clutching Blues Unlimited and Steve Grossman's blues guitar manual: "Ladies and gentlemen, a big hand for that legendary Mississippi blues man—Roebuck Staples"! To sympathetic applause a 60-year-old black man in a baggy suit clutching a battered guitar would shuffle on stage to engross his hairy audience with whining bottleneck blues.**

And when Roebuck wasn't doing a European tour or an occasional $200 gig on campus, or dealing with the latest field researcher who wished him to reminisce on the influence of Robert Johnson, or sing his 12-bar compositions in tiny studios for Negro Arts records who'd press up a 1,000 copies to be snapped up by students in Doug Dobells Folk & Blues Record Shop . . . when Roebuck wasn't doing any of those things, he'd sit in his neat wooden shack and maybe wonder why black kids were no longer interested in the blues.

Instead, a little luck and a vast amount of resilience has decreed a different lifestyle for Roebuck Staples. He wears the slickest duds and when he offers a manicured hand to shake, a large gold ring flashes.

He is, of course, the driving force behind one of soul music's hottest acts and the adulation he encounters is greeted with a predictable downhome philosophy. Yeah, he don't mind rapping over old days, as he picks a piece of thread from the sleeve of his immaculately cut aubergine suit.

"I played the blues and I still dig those old time blues songs. But I've always been a churchman and so it seemed nat'ral to singing gospel. At first I was a gospel singer alone, I was solo, just me and my guitar."

Roebuck was born in Winona, Mississippi on the 28th December 1915. He grew up knowing hard times . . . and the blues. He sang blues and played at neighbours house-parties. But he found the Lord and took to singing at the Local Baptist church.

In 1931 he joined a local spiritual group, the Golden Trumpets. For two years they toured the churches. But times were hard and when the depression started to squeeze the life out of cotton country Pop took his wife Oceola and his two children, Cleotha and Pervis, and moved to Chicago looking for work and a better life. On hitting Windy City he sang with another gospel group, the Trumpet Jubilees when not fighting for a buck.

As the American economy, and the Staples' meagre budget, normalised, Oceola bore two more children: Yvonne, born in '39, and Mavis, one year later. As they grew so did Roebuck's belief in the musical ability of his family. A family gospel group emerged in 1951, prior to which Roebuck had pulled his

family through some empty food cupboard years, not to mention a World War. Roebuck, by now known affectionately as Pop, worked in the car wash, or the stockyard, the construction pit or the steelyard but somehow he hung on in there.

In '51, Pop, playing as mean a blues guitar as in those far off Mississippi days, proudly presented Cleotha, Pervis, and Mavis to a Baptist church congregation. Their sincere, wailing spirit-lifting singing gained a standing ovation and a routine was set: every Sunday the Staples Singers would convert some souls with their music.

Yvonne and Mavis finished school in 1954 and soon the group entered a recording studio for the first time. The Chicago recording scene in the fifties had dozens of small independents hustling for a piece of the 'race market' action and one of them, United Records, recorded the group doing a traditional number "Sit Down Servant".

"It sold about 200 that first thing. They heard us—a lady from the record company and liked us—so we recorded. But the man who owned the company, he wanted us to do rock and roll, we wanted no part of rock and roll. So he held us for two years on contract with that one record. When his contract was up Vee Jay asked us to come and do a record, so we did and that record sold 1,000. The first Vee Jay record we made was "If I Can Get My Brother To Pray Again" and "God's Wonderful Love" and as it sold 1,000 I thought Vee Jay was disappointed with us so we were ready to quit. But Vee Jay said 'no, no, when will you be ready to go into the studio?' And I said, 'I'm ready to go in now.' So we went and we made "Uncloudy Day" and it sold like rock and roll!"

"Uncloudy Day" is a minor classic, a solemn blues figure on Pop's echoing electric guitar, and Mavis' swooping, soaring lead promising a better life one day.

"Uncloudy Day's" success cemented a four-year stay with Vee Jay records. Over those years the 30–40 tracks recorded show a bluesy, fairly inhibited and deeply soulful style which set them apart from most other gospel teams. Although the devices employed (call and response, melismatic lead, emotional climaxes etc.) were those of the standard gospel tradition, the songs, more often than not written by Roebuck, were based on the blues chords of his guitar.

"The whole foundation was a Southern-style, not a Chicago-style. After the first few sides we added a bass (Phil Upchurch) and drums (Al Duncan). "Uncloudy' was our biggest Vee Jay record. "Will The Circle Be Unbroken" about the next and "Help Me Jesus" the third. We made a lot of big sellers big gospel you know."

They also wrote and recorded a song called "This May Be My Last Time," which the Rolling Stones later 'borrowed' for their big hit "The Last Time".

But with Vee Jay unable to produce another record with pop-like sales like "Uncloudy Day", the group moved to a new company. But, surprisingly, they didn't choose one established in the black gospel field.

In 1960 the folk boom was beginning to hootenanny its way across white campuses and overnight anyone who could pluck a banjo and bawl "Frankie And Johnny" was assured of an audience. Some black performers (Josh White, Chambers Brothers, Leon Bibb and Odetta) made good bread singing traditional or quasi-traditional music in student-packed coffee houses. The record industry scrambled to record the phenomenon and one of the leaders in the rush was the jazz and folk outfit Riverside Records.

Riverside, on signing the Staples Singers, proceeded to present the group as an authentic anachronism and soon they were recording the gospel standards ("Didn't It Rain", "Amazing Grace"). The sales weren't as high as Riverside hoped, however, possibly because the couple of dozen sides recorded, with the exception of some disastrous Christmas numbers weren't musically that different from the deeply soulful Vee Jay sides.

1961, and on the Staples Singers moved, this time to the huge Columbia Corporation. At first Epic tried persevering with a 'folk' image but with the quasi-folk bubble bursting and Columbia unfamiliar with marketing black gospel without making it 'respectable' (Mahalia Jackson with strings) they were puzzled to know what to do with such a down-home gospel group.

"Riverside really tried to put us in a folk bag so we could be more commercial so we could sell records but we still didn't quite make it with them. When it didn't work we tried Columbia. Our first producer there, Billy Sherill, couldn't find us either so they brought in Larry Williams."

For years Roebuck had been writing the group's material, bluesy in chord construction, wistful in melody, and devotional in lyrical content. In 1967 Roebuck simply kept the music the same but dropped the more direct references to God in the lyrics. Not that a deeply religious and gospel loving man like Roebuck 'Pop' Staples could blatantly sell out. His songs still retained heavy 'messages' but abstract ones, universal love, let's have peace (after all, in another culture Dylan was proving that the audience for a non-religious sermon was a huge one).

His first 'pop-gospel' song was "Why Am I Treated So Bad" and for its production they called in a soul producer (with a historic rock and roll background), Larry Williams. Now there was a bevy of R&B session men, as well as an echoing guitar to accompany the group. The single made the Hot 100, though only in a minor way, but the song eventually became an R&B standard recorded successfully by Cannonball Adderley and the Sweet Inspirations.

The Staple Singers had taken their first tentative steps into the heady soul world and there was no turning back now. Another Williams production, "For What It's Worth"—coming from the pen of Stephen Stills—proved a soul hit. At last they were beginning to find a young black audience who dug Mavis' wailing lead. So in July 1968 the Staples, complete with Mavis, moved labels for the final time, to the home of Memphis funk.

"The way we got with Stax . . . we knew a young man Al Bell who was a disc jockey and he was crazy about our records. He started running a record company and they called him out of Washington. He started working with Stax, so he knew the group and he dug the group. We signed to Stax, but somebody else produced for us for the first two years, they couldn't find us and we were fixing to split from Stax and then Al said he wanted to produce us."

The 'somebody else' who produced the Staples was Steve Cropper. The first Stax single "Long Walk To DC" was a driving, gutsy record, though a relative sales failure. Stax had been taken over a little time before by the Gulf & Western conglomerate and for a while Stax struggled to find again the midas touch which had made Otis and Sam & Dave household names. The group put out good music and hoped success's pendulum would swing there again. Certainly the two Cropper produced albums had plenty of guts but still the group were presented as folky, down home philosophers . . . and such an image had little wide appeal in the slick soul market.

The difference in Al Bell's production from Steve Cropper's brought the group immediate success. Pervis left the group in 1970 and was replaced by Yvonne who was returning to the Staples fold. Sighs Mavis with a discernible note of admiration in her voice: "Heavy Makes You Happy went really high and we knew Al had the sound we were looking for. We started doing much bigger shows, rock concerts. Al took us down to Muscle Shoals and we were knocked out with the groove those guys could get behind our singing. We just got bigger and bigger. A songwriter in Memphis, Mack Rice, brought this song to us. We listened to it and we just couldn't get it to the studio fast enough. "Respect Yourself" earned us a gold disc of course. It started with the kids, you know they had little slogans saying "Respect Yourself" which they'd attach on the backs of their shirts and stuff."

The dropping of the small 's' in the group's name was of no real significance but the string of huge soul and pop hits that followed was.

Said Mavis: "You know since we become 'stars', whatever that is, it's been pretty hectic and everything moves kinda fast. 'Be What You Are', 'I'll Take You There', 'If You're Ready Come Go With Me'—our records are kinda funky but we still do message songs. But we had to move with the times. Now we try to get across our message to a bigger audience, that's all. Two of our most exciting experiences in recent times have been the 'Soul To Soul' and 'Wattstax' concerts. We can *see* our sound getting to so many people. The first non-gospel songs we ever sung were 'Blowing In The Wind' and 'This Land Is Your Land'."

"I don't think the message in our lyrics has changed since those times. Sure the beat's got harder. But the message is the same."

Black Music Gallery

Staple Singers

Black Music Gallery

Pointer Sisters

Black Music Gallery

O’Jays

# O' Jays

**IN 1958 in every high school in every state of America, students (some with talent, some without) were forming would-be doo-wop groups. Two of five young men in the Canton McKinly High School were Eddie Levert and Walter Williams, who, as the LeVert Brothers, shouted the Lord's praises on a creaking local radio station. With William Powell, Bobby Massey and Bill Isles they sewed stripes down the side of their pants and doo-wahed for anyone who'd listen.**

Enter on this scene of engaging naivity, one "Andreotti" who, with a quick "I'll make you into stars", pushed some of his newly-composed songs into the group's hands and took the group off to New York for an audition with Decca.

Decca were unimpressed, so the group tried a more black-oriented label: Cincinnatti's King Records. Reportedly, Syd Nathan gave them the name of the Mascots on the signing of the contract. They cut eight sides, including 'Do The Wiggle', 'That's The Way I Feel' and 'The Story Of My Heart' at one session and the sides show a young, nervous group, but with a sweet blend of doo-wop harmony and gospelly 5 Keys-ish fervour. However, the songs were nothing, the promotion behind the 2 or 3 released (not until 60–61) was nothing, and the group never saw a King royalty cheque nor a Cincinnatti recording session again.

A few months after the King session they became friendly with a big Cleveland disc jockey, Eddie O'Jay. He helped them get booked for smallish shows in the Cleveland area, took them to a then obscure Detroit producer Don Davis, where they cut 'Miracles' (on Dayco and then leased to Apollo) and gave them a new name—his own. The O'Jays "worked the clubs", polishing their sound as well as the cuffs and elbows of their suits. They were suffering from a serious bout of stagnation when they met up with H. B. Barnum, a West Coast singer/pianist/producer. By 1963, Leiber and Stoller had laid down a set of rules on production which were to dominate R&B for the next few years: strings, tympani, echo chambers and hits. So when H. B. took them to Los Angeles to work as back-up musicians behind Lou Rawls and Jimmy Norman for Barnum's Little Star label, the concept of what a black group should sound like had become as rigid as the doo-wop era they had just left. A Levert/William composition was the O'Jays' first and only on Little Star, and because of his sales movement, H. B. was able to get the group with an R&B giant: Imperial Records. Up until '63 whatever sales their records had had were on

a comparatively regional basis, but now a reflective understated ballad backed by a dramatic overstated accompaniment gave them a small national hit, 'Lonely Drifter'.

The group's Imperial era had a highspot in the soaring vocal acrobatics complete with Tony Williams-like hiccough on 'Stand In For Love'. Yeah, 1965 saw them in pretty good shape.

The following year, however, was a bad one. Imperial was bought out by the Liberty conglomerate who didn't seem interested in a group that, at the whims of Barnum or Nick De Caro, were buried in echo with a sound often more Johnny Moore and the Drifters than the O'Jays. They cut a record for Minit ('Working On Your Case'), which meant little at the time, though with a relentless clomp clomp beat behind the falsetto lead, it has been dubbed a "classic" by Northern disco dwellers. In August, 1966, Bill Isles quit the group and they all moved back to Cleveland, more than a little cheesed off.

By 1967 the inactive quartet were prepared to quit, but instead a couple of Cleveland bigshots, Jules Berger and Leo Frank, offered them the chance of a "comeback" appearance. Leo's Casino gave a show with Chuck Jackson as the headliner, but it was the group who stole the whole show. A business "alliance" was formed (Jules and Leo with the bread, and Bobby Massey, their longtime business manager, with the know-how) and the resulting company, Prime Enterprises, got them a clean break from Liberty/Minit and a new contract. The group had been playing the Apollo in Harlem when disc jockey Rocky Gee persuaded them to cut some demo's with producer Richard King. Gee took the dubs to Larry Uttal who dug them, signed the group to Bell records and brilliantly placed the group with producer George Kerr.

Kerr had served a hard apprenticeship with Motown Records, handling their New York "hits of the shows" albums, but with his roots firmly entrenched in doo-wop brought out a sound of subtle rhythm and harmony. And with good songs from the likes of the Poindexter Brothers, it was hardly surprising that "I'll Be Sweeter Tomorrow" and "Look Over Your Shoulder" were huge soul hits (*and* fairish pop ones). An album came out (with dubbed-on audience ruining it) and the next couple of Bell singles didn't do a lot and

then bang! It happened again—their label got taken over by a giant corporation.

The group, wishing to escape another Imperial hassle, had put a clause in their contract giving them an easy way out and they were soon floating free. Quickly two dudes from Philadelphia moved in to grab the string of the O'Jays' balloon. Philly, like New Orleans, always had a tendency to develop artists and producers with unique and inward-looking ideas. Kenny Gamble and Leon Huff were determined to put a Philly Sound on the map. Their Neptune label brought the O'Jays back to the charts. The group's first Gamble/Huff production "One Night Affair" is a masterpiece of churning, rolling dance music, with a piano-dominated beat. The success of this record was quickly followed by "Branded Bad", "Deeper" and "Looky Looky". But Chess/GRT (who distributed Neptune) ran into financial trouble. It was time to move on yet again . . .

1971 found the group recording in Cleveland for a local company, Saru, where they made a disc with H. B. Barnum: "Peace" (later reissued by Astroscope). In September '71 Bobby Massey quit to "concentrate on production" (indeed the group discovered the Pondersosa Twins + One, who chalked up a million seller with "You Send Me").

1972 was, at last, the time for an O'Jays' million seller. Said Levert, right back in the Neptune days, "we always felt that Kenny and Leon were more able than any other producers to capture the group on record. We had an offer to go with Motown just before we signed to Philadelphia International. They offered us big financial guarantees and such, we just wanted to be the O'Jays and we feel we can accomplish that better with Gamble and Huff."

Their accomplishments have of course been phenomenal. Eddie Levert, Walter Williams and William Powell have come on with some of the best music to come out of any culture, black or white: "Back Stabbers", "992 Arguments", "Love Train", you'd have to live in an igloo to be unaware of those sweet Philly classics. And now you can add to those "Put Your Hands Together", and the pulsating "For The Love Of Money" from their "Ship Ahoy" album. It's been a long road for the O'Jays, but their music has travelled beautifully.

# 3 Degrees

**A discussion of the Three Degree's music is like a discussion of Raquel Welch's acting: bound to miss the essential point of what the subject is all about. If you think the Three Degrees are purely music to listen to you're probably blind and paralysed and maybe even deaf.**

A hearing of the group's Philadelphia International album won't challenge you intellectually but your temperature is likely to rise if you see these delectable temptresses in the flesh, that is if you're male chauvinist, and susceptible to that totally American idea of presenting black female beauty in a superbly tight, sequin flashing cabaret act. When I was ushered into the beautifully smiling ladies I wondered whether they'd be prepared to talk about such trifling things as records when a whole world of beauty hints or who was seen recently on the arm of Engelbert Humperdinck was there for the discussing.

To their total credit Fayette Pickney, Sheila Ferguson and Valerie Thompson, with their legendary manager Richard Barrett, happily unfolded their musical history.

"We all were born and grew up in Philadelphia. The original Three Degrees were Linda Turner, Shirley Porter and me (Fayette Pickney). One day I was playing around on the piano at one of the girl's houses and I'm just singing at the top of my lungs not knowing that it's a producer sitting there, on the couch. After we'd finished messing around he got up and said "I'm Richard Barrett, I'll make you into stars."

"And immediately I sat down with my mouth closed, nothing else to say. He sat at the piano and he played all his hit records, my mouth went 'Oh you wrote that!' Then he asked us if we would seriously like to sing. We said yeah, sure, but he said "Look, music's no game. And it sure wasn't."

"Our first recording was arranged, you see Richard had left New York to come to work for Swan Records in Philly. The first thing we ever cut was "Gee Baby (I'm Sorry)" and it was a hit. Over the next three years or so there were various girls in the group. In all about six to eight different ones. You know because at the time to some girls it was just a fad. To other girls it was just something to do. But in showbusiness you have to be very, very, serious about it. It's very difficult for girls on the road. Guys can go from one city or country to another and just take it over by storm but ladies can't do that, you know. It is a little more difficult.

"We had some quite successful records with Swan. After "Gee Baby" we had "I'm Gonna Need You", "Close Your Eyes"—that's an old 5 Keys song and "Look In My Eyes" a number Richard originally wrote for the Chantels. We also did our first version of the Chantels' "Maybe" for Swan in '66. I guess the company was getting into difficulties after losing the Beatles and all 'cause the last couple of Swan records, those were "Tales Are True" and "Love Of My Life" didn't sell too well. But then we were doing some pretty good night-club work.

"Richard took us to Boston to create and build up our stage work so that if and when we did get a hit record we had an act. Because a lot of groups get a hit and they don't know

Black Music Gallery 3 Degrees

Black Music Gallery — Chi-Lites

the front from the back of the stage. We thought it would really be a feather in our cap to be able to perform and entertain people as well as just singing the record. So that's how we got out on the road working and working and in a year or so we had gained popularity and worked our way up to the largest night-club in Boston. And from there we signed with a major agency and performed in big night-clubs all over the world.

"But you need records for exposure, you can't travel that fast, you know, when you have a hit record your name means something, you can have concerts and you can fill houses with tremendous capacities. Mind, some of the big night-clubs have closed down and now unless you're a superstar you can't really make a lot of money."

As the girls' supper club bookings grew the group, now firmly settled as Fayette, Sheila and Valerie signed with Warner Bros. Records. The stay (a single, "Contact") was brief, as was their stay with Metromedia, where they cut "The Feeling Of Love", among others. Prior to joining the Three Degrees Sheila Ferguson had had a couple of solo records out on Jamie and Swan—"Little Red Riding Hood" was 'a local hit'. The sound of the Three Degrees singles from '65–'68 is much as it is today, rather rigid harmony singing with the arrangements and material, more than the singing, putting the group in a soul bag.

"In 1969 we, or should I say Richard, teamed up with Kenny Gamble and Leon Huff—they and Chess Records had their Neptune label. We had met Kenny and Leon when we were with Swan, they weren't into producing then though they were writing songs all the time. So they and Richard used to collaborate sometimes and they started to get more into producing. They saw us at the Latin Casino in New Jersey and they'd like to record us. We did one track, "What I See" just the one track. They released it and we didn't even know they were going to put it out—a deal was going to be negotiated. But by the time it came out we had already signed with Roulette.

"When we signed with Roulette we did a new version of "Maybe". It was our biggest hit, and a lot of people say our best record. It was the first time we'd ever done a wailing kind of soul thing. Valerie did the lead and that big monologue got to all the girls. It still gets to the girls in the audience when we do it on stage. We did an album with Roulette (Released here on Mojo), some R&B tunes, some standards, some rock, like our cabaret act really.

"Someday we would like to do a live recording, you know, a "Three Degrees On Stage" album. That's where our heart is, on stage. We always want to capture on record what we do on stage. But it's two different worlds. After "Maybe" we tried a whole range of different styles on singles. We did a real funky thing, "You're The One", Sly Stone wrote that first for Little Sister, and "Ebb Tide" the standard. We stayed with Roulette till our contract ran out but we were so busy with so many other things it's surprising we had time to record anything!

"We worked in "The French Connection" movie—that was a big thrill; did some TV commercials and toured with Engelbert Humperdinck. Backing him was a new experience! But we weren't really sorry to leave Roulette and we were really pleased to join Gamble and Huff. "Dirty Old Man" has sold well for us of course and our first album we're very pleased with.

"I suppose some folks will think that because we play to mainly white audience in top clubs we haven't got a feeling for black music. We've got the feeling, we just need the right material. We do play occasionally to black audiences and when Val hits "Maybe" women's hands go up in the air, they scream and they say "yeah, tell me baby!" And when Val says "you know it's really hard to find a guy who'll really blow your mind" she gets about 70 answers out of the audience."

# Chi-lites

**"HELLO, is that Eugene Record?" "No, . . . he's not here right now . . . this is Marshall Thompson . . . the leader of the Chi-Lites."**

The *faux pas* was understandable, Everyone is encouraged to think of Eugene Record as the leader, originator and total controller of the Chi-Lites artistic and commercial destinies. But a group one man does not make. And despite Eugene's brilliance—through his memorable songs, his expressive falsetto lead and above all his towering sound-in-depth productions—the Chi-Lites are a *group* . . . not one creative energy, but four.

Yes, they're four again. "The last time we were over there in England we were just three. But now we have our bass singer Creadel back. Creadel is the guy who did that part-lead on "Power To The People". He retired for about a year. We never did get a replacement in when he was away, we just waited for that music bug to get him again! So it's us four guys on the new album which we've just recorded."

Marshall talks with enthusiasm. A new album out soon, a hit (in the States and Britain) with "Homely Girl", in fact a complete recovery from that slight lull in their royalty cheques. You can't argue with hits like "Stoned Out Of My Mind", "Homely Girl" and the new tip-for-the-top "There Will Never Be Any Peace". The Chi-Lites are ensuring that their brand of Chicago Soul wasn't just a fleeting diversion which began with the mind-blasting "Power To The People" and finished with mesmerising musical montage "The Coldest Days Of My Life". If you've endured the years of playing clubs where a large family would pack the place out and where R&B superstardom seemed far off you're not likely to get *too* discouraged when a couple of singles miss, nor when the critics claim, with partial justification, that re-writings of "Have You Seen Her" were dragging the group into self-parody.

"Yeah, it's been a hard road to travel. You know I was talking to Major Lance recently. When he started out I was his drummer! Yeah, everything has to change in time. I was a drummer, playing at the Regal Theatre. I used to play behind all the big acts. So of course, I got to know a lot of artists, promoters—I was always meeting different people. When I retired from the drums I knew everybody on the Chicago scene so to speak. I always dug the vocal group thing, The Dells, the Flamingos. In fact the whole basis of the group thing now is the groups that were big in the fifties. I knew a bunch of guys from groups. So I formed a new one."

The new group, formed in 1960, besides consisting of Marshall Thompson, born in Chicago in 1941, featured a life-long buddy and fellow Chicagoan Eugene Record (born 1940); Robert Lester born in McComb, Mississippi in 1942 and Creadel Jones born in 1939 in St. Louis, Missouri; plus a fifth member Clarence Johnson. Eugene, Clarence and

Robert, the latter known as "Squirrel", had sung (and even recorded—a single for Renee Records in 1959), with a small-time vocal team the Chantours. Marshall and Creadel had sung together with an even more obscure (and non-recorded) outfit, the Desideros. The quintet called themselves the Hi-Lites and with one of Marshall's 'contacts' Carl Davis producing them hustled a recording contract with Mercury Records. The released disc was called "Pots And Pans" and it's total sales failure might have suggested that the guys were better suited to cleaning them. But they kept going. "We changed our name, we had to because we found there was another group called the Hi-Lites. We figured that if we added a 'C' to the front of our name that'd give us an original name *and* indentity us from coming from Chicago. We did that in '64 when we recorded some little ol' records for James Shelton." In many ways James Shelton Jr. was and is the archtype small-time record producer. From a tiny office in a Chicago back-street he runs his Daran and Ja-Wes labels recording a bit of blues (Big John Wrencher), a bit of jazz (The Counterpoints), and some soul. The Hi-Lites' "I'm So Jealous" on Daran was a happy sounding dance disc which skipped with the "Chicago beat" that a wave of producers and arrangers were developing for Columbia's Okeh records.

The group became Marshall and The Chi-Lites and "Love Bandit" became a sizable Chicago breakout, without Shelton showing the aptitude nor the resources to push it into national charts. A third disc, this time, just the Chi-Lites, eventually came out on Ja-Wes "You Did That To Me", but by that time Mercury had signed the group once again. "I'm So Jealous" was put out nationally on Blue Rock in January '65. The group got ready for their first national tour, Then . . . nothing. Somehow the hit wasn't to be and a new record on Blue Rock "Ain't You Glad Winter's Over" meant even less. Yeah, '65 promised much but gave little.

The Chicago scene continued to inwardly develop its own brand of unsinuating soul music and so it was to the local, and not the national scene that the Chi-Lites relied on to pay the grocery bills. A production company Dakar had sprung up in the Windy City and in 1967 Marshall and The Chi-Lites had "Price Of Love" out on Dakar Records—their first release. Lack of distribution, and a meandering musical direction meant little sales. But Dakar, with heavy 'name' producers in their driving seat were soon able to get a deal with a national label—MCA. The Music Corporation Of America were beginning to dabble in R&B, after years of country and middle of the road, and launched their Uni and Revue R&B labels. Dakar got a leasing deal, and Revue 11005 gave the world, or a tiny segment of it, the lilting "Love Is Gone". The group had finally settled for the name the Chi-Lites. In 1968 they also settled for the Brunswick label. Eugene Record was pushed to the front as songwriter/producer. "1969 was when we first made it. We had a hit (number 10 in the Billboard R&B chart) with "Give It Away". We went and brought some new suits, went out on the road. All of a sudden a record company was interested in us. Eugene was getting some big successes with Barbara Acklin. Eugene was always a good writer. Some of the things we record now he wrote years ago when he was a nobody." Eugene's writing was only half the story. His productions, with their liberal use of strings, fuzz guitar, deep billowing bass lines and 'full' sounding vocals gave the group an original sound, a sound rewarded with hits ("Let Me Be The Man My Daddy Was", "The Twelfth Of Never" in 1969, "24 hours of Sadness", "I Like Your Lovin' (Do You Like Mine)" and "Are You The Woman (Tell Me So)" in 1970). All they needed was a pop super-smash. They got it in 1970.

"We all figured that we needed to broaden our sound. Up until then we'd choose mainly ballads. Sweet things. There was a lot of unrest and injustice in the world and we all felt that artists couldn't ignore that situation and sing just about love. So Eugene wrote this uptempo number called "(For God's Sake) Give More Power To The People". We worked on it a long time. Creadel sang this big bass line, and the rhythm track was put down by Eugene just about by himself. He played guitar, bass and keyboards. That moog intro was the final touch. We *knew* it'd be a big one."

"Power To The People" became a smash soul, pop and eventually international hit, and clocked up the statutory millionth sale essential for a 'stardom' description to ring true. Their follow up "We Are Neighbors" despite a coy-'comedy' intro had a similarly aggressive dance beat guaranteed to vibrate the body's lower regions. Wisely the group changed style, and pace, for a new single in mid 1971 with "I Want To Pay You Back (For Loving Me)". A lyric of crushing sacherine-sweetness, but a beautiful, lilting sound. The mood and images of woman's-magazine-love-stories were explored further with their next single.

"We went on tour with Barbara Acklin and Gene Chandler in 1970. Eugene and Barbara just sat down and came up with this song "Have You Seen Her". We all wanted to record it but Eugene kind of reckoned it was too long, you know, not really commercial. Eventually we did it on the "Power To The People" album and with that big spoken bit nobody saw it as a single and certainly not a hit. So you can imagine how we felt when it came out as a 45 . . . and went and sold over two million."

The sentimentality of "Have You Seen Her" to some extent obscured the disc's charm, and its phenomenal success brought several other numbers from the prolific pen of Mr. Record which relied entirely on "Have You" for melody and arrangement. But their copies were mainly tucked away on albums. The Chi-Lites' next single "Oh Girl" with its wistful, dreamy melody and a drifting, harmonica intro was another aspect of their sound, another smash. The group, through skilful use of multi-tracking had a rich reservoir of sound which, if not the well spring of spontaneous creativity, gave a suitable harmonic base of lushness in which Eugene's hesitant, poignant tenor wallowed with the appropriate degree of suggested sincerity.

"Our arrangers, Tom Tom Washington, Willie Henderson and Sonny Sanders are obviously very important to us. So are the musicians we use, Quinton Joseph is a fine drummer. We try to plan it so that our singles never follow a standard pattern. Some are fast ("We Need Order" an over-orchestrated an somewhat passé attempt at social statement) and some are slow ("Letter To Myself" a rather beautiful wallow in self-pity). For a while last year people said we were in a rut, but Eugene came up with a song which hit our critics in the face ("Stoned Out Of My Mind", a joyful, electro-synthesized, deftly mellow, dance exhortation about getting high on love not grass). "The Chi-Lites" album (just released in Britain by Decca) is easily our best LP released so far. We were able to put a lot of extra work in on the vocals and Eugene has learned so much about getting the sounds he wants in the studio. Yeah, I suppose you could say our records are meticulously put together. The lead track will be the single for us. It's called "There Will Never Be Any Peace Until God Has"? It's got to be one of the best tunes we've ever recorded. Also on the album will be a song B. B. King has cut "I Like To Live The Love I Sing About". Like B. B. is a blues singer, but when I heard the song I knew we would have to do a version.

"You know it would be nice to get into more and more kinds of music. Like we did a country and western thing ("My Heart Just Keeps On Breakin'" with a steel guitar rating incongrously but delightfully behind the group's joyous vocal) and we'd like to continue to experiment. But you know you've got to give the people what they want to hear as well. Now we're stars, we can work on various ideas, but it's the people who buy the records, who mould our sound. And on stage we do all our old recordings because a lot of people have got memories of those old songs. When we come to Britain we won't disappoint our fans. Did you see us when we came to Britain last time? You did? Well you *know* the Chi-Lites gave the fans what they want."

Marshall was laughing now. But it was a very confident laugh from the leader of the Chi-Lites.

# Thom Bell

**THOM Bell smiles a lot. And it isn't only his natural good humour which creases his handsome, bearded face into another explosion of laughter. Over ten million sellers as a producer, arranger and writer makes Thom a vital part of the Philly Legend. If it wasn't for this modest, instantly likable man the Delfonics, the Stylistics, the Detroit Spinners, Ronnie Dyson and New York City would be unknown to the mass audience.**

Yet Thom looks upon himself as a lucky man whose talents have been handsomely rewarded in a world where talent often brings no reward save the knowledge of artistic integrity . . . and that's difficult to eat. No, even as a kid Thom had good breaks.

"I had a terrific childhood, I was born in Philadelphia but my folks are from the West Indies. They made it to the United States before I was even a gleam in my father's eye.

"We were middle-class I guess. We weren't in the worst shape . . . but then we weren't in the best shape. We couldn't eat steak all the time but we didn't eat beans all the time either. My father is an accountant. I never liked school. When I was five I started playing the piano, when I was six I started studying . . . I mean in order to survive in my house if you were gonna learn something you had to learn it the right way—there was no way out. Then I took to drums also—So when I was eight I was studying piano *and* drums at the same time. I took that for about a year but I didn't sorta like the drums that well and by the time I was nine I took the flugelhorn and piano.

"I heard my first music other than classical when I was about 14. The first things I dug were by the Flamingos, they had "Where Or When". I used to hear a bit of the Platters before that. And Tommy Edwards . . . he had "It's All In The Game". My father had the Platters things, later he had Elvis Presley's "Return To Sender" I used to hear that 1,000 times. One of my best school buddies then was Kenny Gamble, we were writing together since we were 15 years of age. When I was a young kid my ears were only really attuned to the classics, but I was beginning to change. Kenny went to school with my sister, you see we went to two different high schools. My sister Barbara was my twin, we were two of a family of ten. Anyway, Kenny went to school with Barbara. I think he was a little sweet on her at the time . . . if my memory serves me correct . . . and she was a little sweet on him. He didn't play, he was a singer."

When Thomas Bell was studying lithography at college, Bernie Lowe was studying Philadelphia as a possible base for his record label. And when the Cameo and Parkway labels emerged they helped squeeze the last breaths of life from the pure rock and roll form of the golden fifties with first Charlie Gracie, and later, Bobby Rydell pouring good looks and emasculated music into the rock singer's mould. But it was when Chubby Checker twisted the neck of vocal group R&B that Philadelphia became the place for hits. And so it was to the Cameo building that Tommy and Kenny headed for when they left school in 1959. As Kenny Gamble explained:

"The doors weren't opened to get in to Cameo at that time. But Jerry Ross was a guy who was in the Shubert Building also on the sixth floor. Me and Tommy came to see the guy in 1959. We were singing together as a duet, Kenny and Tommy. We recorded a record on Jerry's label, Heritage Records. It was a bomb, it went nowhere."

But if the disc "Some Day" sold nothing at least it introduced the teenagers to the heady world of records. In 1960 the duo became a quintet and Kenny & Tommy became Kenny Gamble and The Romeos, the other Romeos being Roland Chambers (guitar), Winnie Walford ("he was the bass player but he's an actor now"), and Carl Chambers (drums). By the early sixties Thom was getting some session work with Cameo and soon the Romeos were makin' tracks too. Thom chuckles when he searches his memory bank.

"I went over to Cameo for an audition when Chubby Checker walked into the room. I was working on my tunes to make sure they were right before presenting them to the people at Cameo. Chubby was in the habit of walking in on anybody, he likes to see what's going on, he's a real nosey guy. So he says "let me hear your song". So I play the song and he likes it so he says "would you like to write for me?" Oh yeah! Big Chubby Checker. Yeah, sure Mr. Checker. A week later I get a contract. But I didn't write any songs for him. He had me writing for other artists, I wrote a couple of raggy little tunes. But they weren't so hot so I guess we were even. I worked a bit on Cameo sessions. And in 1966 I came to Britain with Chubby, who was on the wane then, as his conductor. The first record I played on was by Bobby Sherman. In fact I used to sing background over Bobby Sherman records . . . yeah background singer. You see you have to supplement your money so I was a background singer and piano player. At that time Cameo were into good-looking Italian boys who really didn't have to sing. But then Motown got big things changed. The Romeos, we became a house band. But we was just the second-string rhythm section. We weren't on any *hits* there at all, because we were just up and coming and, you see, we were just the younger guys. The Motown situation was so big that Cameo had the bright idea of getting an all black rhythm section to play that kind of music. That was simple, all I had to do was hear the record—that was the simplest part. But that wasn't really my forte either, I got a bit bored with that, I never liked copying."

Between sessions backing Cameo-alsorans, the Romeos, backing Kenny Gamble, began working the clubs.

"We used to make a few colleges like Boston, Baltimore, Maryland, but nothing really big. We never wanted to make it so big. We just wanted to make a few hundred dollars a week doing what we liked to do . . . which was playing . . . We did O.K. locally. We were always smart enough to get paid in *advance.* Have to contribute that to Kenny Gamble, he was always the business man, and he's smart to this day. But a lady named Sybil, from Newport, New Jersey, came along and swiped me from the band. Sybil and I got married. So Leon Huff came in."

But by 1966 the band had folded completely. The handful of discs the Romeos, without Thom, cut for Philly's Top DJ, Jimmy Bishop—on his Artic label—(including the regional breakout "Ain't It Baby") are left for Northern stompers boogaloo to. Thom, still remaining faithful to Cameo, who finally crashed in 1967 was about to take a big step to eventual stardom.

"About six months before Cameo closed a fellow called Stan Watson came to me with a group called the Delfonics. He knew nothing about recording, and I really didn't know anything about producing, but it was something that I wanted to learn. I had an idea that I could produce records. Stan Watson brought the group to me. I liked the group pretty good and he said "can you do anything with them? I don't know anything about producing records". So I said "I think I can do the job". So I produced the Delfonics for Cameo. But Cameo didn't like the record. So they sold it to another company called Moonshot and Cameo distributed Moonshot.

"The first record came out called "He Don't Really Love You". Cameo didn't know about the black end of records, the black distributorship and rackjobbing, that's altogether a separate entity in itself. So, "He Don't Really Love You" did well in Phila-

delphia, it did well in one or two other markets, but Cameo didn't want to do it. So I said O.K. I'll produce another one (called "You've Been Untrue"), that one came out on Cameo. And that one got a little bigger . . . but then they lost it again. And then Cameo folded . . . and so did Moonshot.

"So when all the contracts were handed back to the artists, Stan Watson said "Listen I think we should try again, but this time we should try with our own label". So Stan Watson formed Philly Groove Records and he asked me if I'd go with them and I said sure . . . I had nothing else to do . . . there was no more Cameo. So we went to the Cameo Studios, they still kept the studios, the people who bought it leased the studios out to outside producers. Philly Groove Records was a little raggedy office on 52nd and Spruce Street. We didn't have any air conditioning or anything . . . it was hot . . . boy I used to rehearse in my teeshirt and my bermuda shorts and sandals . . . if it was a 100 outside it was a 105 inside. That was '67.

"La La Means I Love You" was Philly Groove's very first thing. That was my third arrangement—arranging for strings and horns. Of course "La La" was a tremendous smash—a million seller. Yeah, I was tickled, that is, once I realised what I'd done. On it I played all the keyboards, and also played the timpanies. I play most of the instruments we couldn't afford to have anybody else play. The other musicians on the disc were the same guys as we use now; Ronnie Baker on bass, Norman Harris on guitar, Roland Chambers, Earl Young and Vince Montana."

Tommy had now officially become Thom and with the Nation's number one under his belt no one was arguing. Thom has somehow mixed an unlikely brew, pure falsetto lead harmony singing, tight rhythm section and lush quasi-classical orchestrations into a hit makers' cocktail. The music world waited with bated breath and poised pen and cheque book to see what followed. What followed, of course, was hit after hit. "I'm Sorry" made No. 42, Hot 100, "Break Your Promise" 35, and even a re-issued "He Don't Really Love You" gave a reactivated Moonshot a small national hit. And when the lush ballad sound became jaded he gave the group an infectious dancer "Ready Or Not Here I Come".

"Yeah, the french horns and flugelhorns and things surprised some folks. In fact on all the sessions I do—even today—the instrumentation is strange. That's the classical training. I wrote songs with the Delfonics' William Hart. He wrote the lyrics. He was good. I didn't do many sessions with Philly Groove and I cut the whole of each track at the same session. I carried 40 pieces into the studio. They had over ten hits. But my mind kept on wanting to lead me somewhere else and where your mind leads you your body is going to go. I knew that I had done as much as I could do with the Delfonics. So I decided to leave Philly Groove. But I didn't get into no fisticuffs thing with Stan Watson."

So Thom Bell left Philly Groove and moved in . . . with Gamble and Huff.

"Gamble asked me if I wanted to come down there with Leon Huff. I said well I don't mind man. I'd known them a long time and they were honest fellows. I said, I'll give it a try. At that particular time they were doing some independent work, they were doing the Intruders for their own label, and they were working with the boys on Crimson, the Soul Survivors.

"They had about three arrangers there but they were looking for one that gave them a different kind of sound. So when I came there the first things I started doing with them was the Jerry Butler stuff: "Never Gonna Give You Up", "Only The Strong Survive", "Western Union Man" things like that. I became their arranger down there for about two years. Jerry came from Chicago down to Philadelphia. Every artist that we had always came to Philadelphia because we were trying to break the Philadelphia scene, it was our own studios. I really dug working with Jerry Butler.

"Then we worked with Dusty Springfield. Yeah she came to Philly. In fact I wrote a hit song for her. That's when Linda Creed and I came into it. That was the first song we'd ever written together, that was a tune called "Free Girl" and it did fairly well—top 70 I think. We were tickled pink. Again, that was the first time we'd ever written together. She was a singer on Philly Groove Records . . . but she wasn't really that hot. She never had a record out, we just took her in the studio one time and tried her but it didn't really sound very good. For some reason she sang but she didn't quite sing well enough. There are singers and there are *singers.* "Linda's a beautiful girl, a French Jew . . . When I left there they gave her her papers back. Linda was born in the States but her father's people are from France. So one day she had a bright idea of writing songs . . . no she wrote poetry. Now I wasn't really in to the poetry thing. So I said "can you write songs?" And she says "I don't know, I never tried." So I said I'll tell you what I'll do, I'll write a melody let's hear you put the lyrics to it. She said O.K. We've been doing it ever since, I'm writing melodies and she's putting lyrics to them. I write the melodies and the sing-a-long, the chorus, of the song. I tell her what I want the song to be about. I do that 85 per cent of the time, then sometimes I just write the melody and she comes up with the chorus. After "Free Girl" Gamble/Huff put her on the staff."

As an arranger Thom Bell proved himself a perfect partner at translating exactly the type of instrumentations and sounds needed to keep Gamble/Huff moving ever forward. As an arranger he had it made, but in this age soul is controlled by the producer.

"A black promotion man I know called me early one morning, I blew that guy out too boy, I said 'Hell, what do you wake me up at 7 o'clock in the morning for?' I had babies man, running all over the house, I wasn't getting much sleep anyway. He told me Avco were after me to produce a group they'd just signed, the Stylistics. The money looked kinda nice. Avco had bought Sebring Records to get the group and their first hit "You're A Big Girl Now" was on the chart. So I said 'I think I can do something with the group, they sound pretty decent.'

"About "You're A Big Girl Now": that kinda music doesn't knock me out. So when I got the group the first thing I did was lower his (Russell Thompkins') voice. When you start singing that high and loud you don't make sense, you just make noise. Now that boy sings *up there* he goes *way up there.* But you're not singing, it's what they call a monotone—monotone means you can sing up or down but you always sound the same. So far I hadn't failed with anything I'd done so Avco were willing to take that chance. The one thing about Russell is that he has a fantastic memory, he can do an album in three hours. He'll sing a song almost the exact way you sang it to him. Fantastic memory. So you don't have to rehearse him for a long time. I rehearsed them ten tunes in 4 hours.

"For their first session the Stylistics needed an hour a side. The first thing was "Stop Look And Listen". And when that did well I said all right, now we have to do an album. So the second time I recorded them I did "Betcha By Golly Wow" and "You Are Everything" . . . and "People Make The World Go Round". People dig the electronic phaser on "You Are Everything" I really enjoy using electronic instrumentation."

The series of hits for the Stylistics has of course run unabated. "I'm Stone In Love With You", "Point Of No Return" and "Rockin' Roll Baby" are familiar to all save the unsavable. Last year Thom was tempted to Atlantic Records to produce the Spinners. Two of the first four sides cut on the group "I'll Be Around" and "Could It Be I'm Falling In Love" have all gone gold, while their "One Of A Kind" has done the same. A year ago Spinner's manager Buddy Allen suggested that Thom direct the flagging career of one-time Hair protégé Ronnie Ryson onto the road of hits. Ronny's "One Man Band" smash was the scintillating result. And it's that hit which cemented his production association with Columbia Records that has subsequently resulted in, amazingly, Johnny Mathis sessions.

"That was another idea I had, uh, I've been trying for three years to get ahold of Johnny Mathis but the company they might have thought that I wasn't right for him. I thought that Mathis is a trend setter, not a trend follower. He has a *fantastic* voice man. I had an *idea* for him for putting him into today's sound . . . but not *funky* now. Just putting him into what's going on today. And piece by piece in the course of the year make him a *leader* again. But "I'm Coming Home" is not what'd I'd call a soul record."

As an independent producer Thom is as sought after as any man, white or black, on the U.S. scene. He's right (New York City—RCA) and very occasionally wrong (Little Anthony—Avco) and retains an almost unique hit-after-hit track record. His latest projects are a songwriting workshop (Joe Jefferson, Vinny Barrett, Melvin and Mervin Steele and Yvette Davis) and the Columbia distributed Tommy label. Tommy the label has yet to really get off the ground due to an enwebbing mesh of contracts which need time to unravel. There'll be a duo Derek & Cindy Floyd "they're kinda black middle-of-the-road", and Thunder "the first girl act I've worked with." And of course, the Spinners, New York City and the Stylistics will still dip regularly into the Thom Bell song and production hitbin.

"I spend a lot of time gettin' the sound worked out in my head. We are using the same musicians but we are not using the same songs, we are not using the same singers. One reason why Gamble/Huff have had me there as an arranger was to sort of calm their rhythms down a bit, sort of add a classier sound against their funky rhythm. They weren't into French horns, English horns, oboes and bassoons and that's why I came into the picture.

"You see, my idea in the whole of my recording career is to learn as much as you can about something, then use that as a stepping stone and go to the next thing, but still retain what's been learned. So when you move up you'll be wiser. That's how I was able to jump from the Delfonics, to the Stylistics then to the Spinners. I feel with my career that I've been real lucky.

"The part that makes me feel good? The money part is fine and the recognition part is fine but the part that really makes me feel good is the realization that what comes out of my head works."

# Bill Withers

**"I don't think I'm further removed now from the type of life I sung about in 'Harlem' than I was before I started singing. Once you've been poor you can never be removed from it. Anyway I've never starved, I've always worked. I've never sat somewhere and waited for someone to send me a cheque. It was just something I wanted to say, I don't have to tell anybody about Harlem, they know it's there."**

Bill Withers has never lived in Harlem, so not being there now is no different from when he wrote the song. He's from a little town called Slab Fork in West Virginia. Being a successful singer does not, he contends, prevent him from being able or willing to write about the inadequate standards of living that Harlemites encounter. So was it the fact that he's black that inspired him to write 'Harlem' and would enable him to continue writing such songs whenever he felt the need?

"There's never any time in my life that I don't remember that I'm black. I look at the world like this. I've got two choices, I can crawl into a hole and feel sorry for myself or I can take a chance and get as much out of life as I can. I would rather take the chances. A lot of people would say 'I don't wanna go to Mississippi 'cause I'm afraid.' I wanna go! I wanna know what's going on down there.

"Sure! 'Harlem' is a song that nobody would assume the writer of it wasn't black, but by the same token anybody can have a grandmother, anybody can be in love. In other words I don't want anybody to con me into believing that the only things that I can write about are those which only black people can

understand. That's not being fair to yourself, that's shutting yourself off from the rest of the world. These are some things that I might write about that are influenced by my being black, but there are also things that are an influence because I'm a human being.

"I wanna be able to write about what everybody else can write about. That's equality! If all you want me to write about is the ghetto then you ain't being fair to me. If you want other people to be interested in black people and understand you, then you've got to want to give some understanding to somebody else, that's how people learn about each other. It's not fair for you to say you understand me and for me to say I don't care about you. You're as many times over a person as the amount of people you understand. I want to understand everybody I can, it's my right as a writer to write about anything that I can think."

Bill Withers hit stardom at the first attempt with 'Grandma's Hands' and 'Ain't No Sunshine' which earned him a gold record in 1970. And he has remained at the top since then with the hits 'Lean On Me', 'Use Me' and 'Kissin' My Love'. Bill who now lives in Benedict Canyon LA. California with his wife Denise Nicholas, had been in the navy for about nine years. On leaving, he took a job as a milkman for a while then joined IBM as a computer operator, and then a job installing toilets with Lockheed Aircraft. Then he decided he wanted to make some music and have some fun.

"I took some of my money, recorded myself and took the tapes around. Some record companies liked me and some didn't but I wound up with Sussex which is owned by a black guy named Clarence Avant, which influenced me some."

Bill says that he never had any musical influences (though he likes listening to Stevie Wonder and Donny Hathaway) and that in fact people originally tried to discourage him from pursuing a musical career since he had never done any singing before. But he was satisfied with the sessions and the way his first album 'Just As I Am' (which was produced by Booker T. Jones) turned out.

"I just played and sung, I never learned music. I don't know how to play anything but I can figure out what I want. I'm not a guitar player, singing is just something I felt I could do, everybody sings.

Bill Withers

Stevie Wonder

"Many things that I had learned in the navy served me well outside. I learned how to organise, I learned leadership and supervision which is what I have to do now. I have to organise a band and produce records which needs a certain amount of leadership and making decisions. On stage I just like to talk to people, I don't wanna go out there and be stiff and unfriendly. Some nights I just don't say anything it depends on how I feel. I just try to stay a human being rather than try to become a performer with an act."

Bill and his band came over to England for a live date at the Rainbow Theatre recently. As far as gigs were concerned Bill had been inactive since the 'Live At Carnegie Hall' date. And Ray Jackson, Bobbye Hall, and James Gadson were missing from the band which made such an excellent tight funky sound at Carnegie Hall. Yet although the Rainbow gig for me was only 'lukewarm' the audience's reaction was great.

"Probably the most satisfying thing to me is that I get some old people, some young people, some black people some white people, guys with long hair, I get all types of people coming to see me. I don't feel like I'm some kind of brilliant person or anything like that, I just make some music y'know, some people like it and some don't. But I wanna be like I am, and I realise that being that way I'm gonna take a risk whenever I step out in front of people. Maybe nobody will like my new songs but what am I gonna do? I've still gotta live."

It has been over a year since the release of the last studio album 'Still Bill', but Bill has just completed an LP of new material.

"I'm not a prolific writer, I just write about anything I can think about, any songs I can make I'm thankful for. I don't know if there will be any difference between the last studio LP and the new one, it's hard to tell about your own music. I can't say that this week I'm gonna write about personal songs and next week I'm gonna write political songs. I'm not that heavy! And you know what? I don't believe anybody else is either. After people do things they say well I did this because of so and so. I would hate to write songs about the same things all the time, I wanna be broader than that."

So, has Bill ever written a song or made any live performances because of any political motivation or partiality?

"I do benefits all the time, I do them for the mayor, I might go do benefits for some

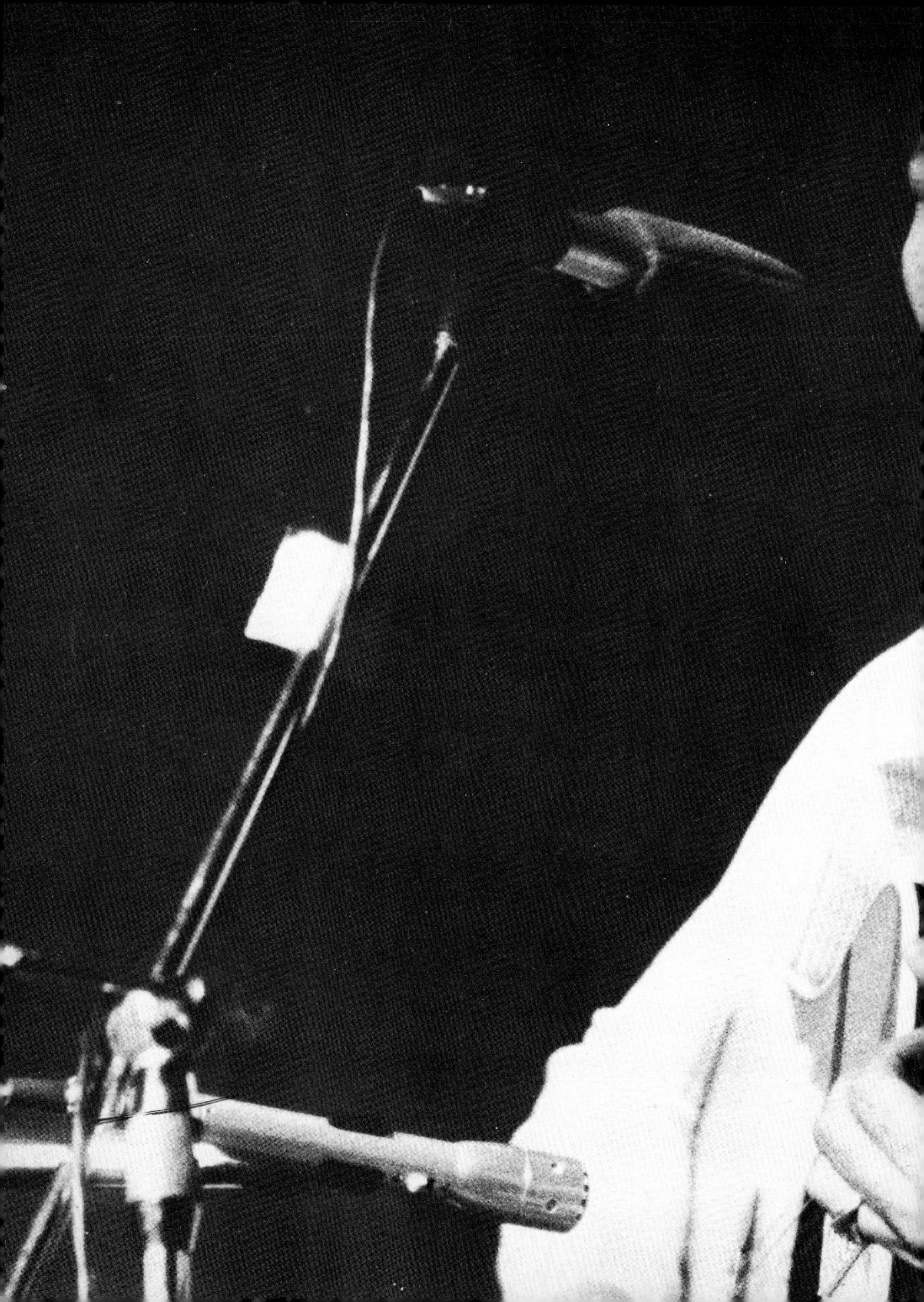

congressman that I wanted to get elected. So far I've been lucky, everybody I've helped have gotten elected. But music is one thing and politics is another, most songs are about three minutes long, you don't have time to say enough in there that would benefit anybody. I make music for pleasure I can't get anybody elected in a song, some people are capable of that maybe I'm not, maybe I'm too ignorant."

One of the things that has taken up Bill's time during the past six months has been acting. He plays a truck driver in a regular American TV series.

"It wasn't something I pursued. They just asked me if I wanted to do it and I said yeah! I think it might be fun. But one reason why I went into it is because everytime you see a black guy in movies you see naked ladies. So I want to do something clean cut. I've liked some black movies, like 'Sounder' and 'Lady Sings The Blues' was a great movie, but some of them are junk, but then a lot of 'white movies' are junk, junk is junk! Some of these black movies that you've seen I had been offered their filmscores but I didn't like the films so I refused them although they would probably have furthered my career. I'd like to score a film that has something in there to write about."

On the question of his overnight success and its effect on him, Bill asserted that there was no personality change only a change in roles, and after all he had been taking new jobs ever since leaving the navy.

"I don't need a screwdriver in my pocket anymore, I have a guitar now. There are things like paying other people's salaries or hiring and firing people that I have to take care of that I didn't have to before. I find it easier to hire somebody than to fire somebody but you still have to function, I'm an employer now. I'm no longer an employee, my record company can't make me do anything. They have a thing and I have a thing. They don't tell me what to do, I make my music the way I want to and I have to solve my own problems."

Bill Withers has a simple and direct musical style and an equally uncomplicated approach to life. He says he wants to remain 'just as he is'. He's aware of the 'down to earth' reputation that the press has given him and he lives up to it whenever he gets the opportunity to sneak up and speak out.

"Sometimes people write things about that you like and sometimes things that you don't like but what are you gonna do? Hide in a hole? You have to stand up to life and challenge it and you have to be honest."

# Pointer Sisters

**IF you've heard their single 'Yes We Can Can' then you'll have experienced a small sample of the extraordinary sounds that Ruth, Anita, Bonnie, and June Pointer make with their voices. Their first LP demonstrated their incredible versatility.**

The remarkable pace at which they sing and scat is immediately the striking aspect of their music. They do so in perfect harmony, the four voices blending as one with urgency feeling and melody. Great soul singers are able always to communicate, through their involvement and enthusiasm, every ounce of emotion in a song. The Pointer Sisters are in that category. And this music along with their 'forties' image has captured the imagination of the American music world where they were suddenly transformed into stars after three years on desperation row.

The Pointer Sisters: Ruth 29, Anita 26, Bonnie 24, and June who is 20, are from Oakland California where they first sang together in the local Church of God.

Bonnie: "We were all baptised into the Church and were there all the way until we got to do what we wanted to do. We had to participate because our father was the Pastor so we had to be involved in everything, to set the example."

Oakland California is a predominantly black area, was it an all black church?

Ruth: "Yeah, but it was run by whites. The authority and the headquarters of the church were all white people and it sort of irritated me because they had a different cultural background from us. They were quiet and . . . (she goes into a low hum to demonstrate the sounds made in the white churches) there wasn't enough activity, it was really stiff. We always wanted to venture out and sing some gospel and . . ."

Bonnie: "Play some tambourines but we never could 'cause they didn't sing those kind of songs. You can't play a tambourine to a ballad, you know!"

How did the professional singing start?

Bonnie: "I just started singing by myself, June was in school and Anita was a legal secretary. That was about five or six years ago, I just sang R&B stuff y'know, any material I found that I liked. I had a friend who played guitar and I used to sing around with him in clubs in Oakland, then my younger sister June joined. Anita joined shortly afterwards and Ruth was the last to join." Ruth: "It seemed like a good idea to me, they seemed to be having a good time and I sure wasn't. I was a key punch operator at the time."

Ruth joined in September '72 which is when the four sisters started working on their first album. But Anita, June and Bonnie had been doing background singing for three years, just oohs, aahs, and yeahs for people like Elvin Bishop, Esther Phillips, Taj Mahal, and Boz Scaggs, who they toured around with. In fact they came to England last summer with Dave Mason and played at the Grosvenor House. All that time they had been gathering songs—self compositions—like 'Sugar' and 'Jada' on the LP.

Bonnie: "That's my sister Anita's little girl (Jada), we wrote the songs together. It was weird how it happened I mean none of us play instruments and Jada was coming over from my mother's house across the bay from San Francisco. She was coming over to Oakland to visit her mother and we just said oh Jada's coming home and all of a sudden the song was born. It's just a true story you know!"

Their sudden transformation to stars was brought about with the release of the album—'The Pointer Sisters' on the Blue Thumb label—which was produced by David Rubinson, the guy who had rescued them three years before after they had gone to Houston with great hopes and with a manager who as it turned out later was no help at all to them. It was Rubinson who had provided the sisters initially with the session work as background singers.

Bonnie: "We were stuck in Houston Texas

*Anita, Ruth, June, Bonnie*

with no money. I had a card that a friend had laid on me in case of an emergency and it was David Rubinson. So I rang him up and said help, no money, get us back to California or get us out of Texas. He'd never heard us sing, he didn't know who I was and here was this person calling him long distance y'know saying help. But he took a chance and sent us our plane tickets and here we are."

But it wasn't until the sisters were rediscovered by Flip Wilson—they appeared on his show to rave reviews—that things had really begun to happen for them. In fact before that, Anita, June, and Bonnie (Ruth had not yet joined) had recorded some sessions for Atlantic Records who had issued an R&B styled single. But that too had been an unsuccessful trip.

What type of audience do they get?

Ruth: "All kinds, it depends on where we are. Back East like Philadelphia and Washington it's a black majority, but most other places it's a white majority audience."

They get a lot of gays in their audiences too, don't they?

Bonnie: "We do. They love it 'cause they get to dress up in tuxedos and . . ."

Ruth: "They can dress up in drag and nobody will ever know (laughs!). A lot of them, they just come to the shows to see what we're gonna have on you know! We're really unpredictable because the forties was fun but that's not where we're headed, we don't aim to stay in these kind of clothes."

How do black people relate to their image?

Bonnie: "We get a lot of fan mail saying that they love it. I love it because it's got class and we can walk in any city as singers and be respected. I've seen rock groups that people just hate to see 'em come into their hotels or their restaurants just because of the image y'know—dope scene and all that. And just by putting on dresses and high heel shoes again instead of jeans and no shoes at all or sandals, they seem to respect you a lot better. And I really like that part 'cause I enjoy being a lady y'know whereas today it seems that a lot of women have forgotten what really being feminine is like. This women's lib thing has really gone crazy."

The Pointer Sisters sing all kinds of music, but is it necessarily black music?

Ruth: "I don't know what it is 'cause I like all kinds of music. I like black music, but I don't like all black music, especially the revolutionary stuff. And the identity singing y'know—I'm singing because I'm black. You don't have to tell anybody you're black . . ."

Bonnie: "Once you know it yourself then that's all that matters, you don't have to keep convincing yourself. Once you know yourself who you are then you don't have to keep singing about it."

Do you ever get any kind of rebuff from black people?

Ruth: "Yup, all the time. They wanna know, are you doing this for the people? Why y'all wearing them long dresses, and why do you wear straight hair? And whenever they asked when is your next tour and I said well we're planning to go to Europe, they said well when are you going to Africa to sing? God! Well whenever I can y'know but going to different countries isn't as easy as they think.

"But I realised I was black when I was very young, it's hard enough but I enjoy life anyway and I'd rather sing about the happier things in life than to sing about the hardships and the struggles and the slavery you know? I mean after all I can't go back and undo all that so I like to sing about things that'll maybe make people forget for a minute. I think that's probably why we love so much comedy 'cause we really love acting silly and crazy sometimes."

Bonnie: "Aren't you gonna ask us if we're really sisters (laughs)? Everywhere we go the first question they ask is if we're really sisters."

Aren't you?

Ruth and Bonnie together (in perfect harmony): "Yes we are."

# Barry White

**THE interview with Barry White was going well, then I nearly blew it.**

Q: "Do you think you owe a lot stylistically to Isaac Hayes?" (Long pause)

A: "No, and about two million people don't think so either."

And he's right. All those critics who dubbed Barry White a mere Hayes plagiarist after hearing the slow tracks on the "I've Got So Much To Give" album, or a one-hit wonder after his second 20th Century single didn't sell as startlingly as his first, have ceased to retain credibility.

Barry might possess the voice least likely to succeed but the multi-digit figures beside titles like "Never Never Gonna Give You Up", "Love Theme" and "Stone Gon'" on 20th Century royalty statements emphatically show it's the producer who's the creative controller, and therefore the dollar earner, of modern-day soul.

"I was born in Galveston, Texas, 1944 though I spent most of my life in Los Angeles. My mom did a bit of acting, she was in a movie "Trader Horn". When I was ten she took me to church and I sang in the choir. When I was 16 I joined an R&B band but they didn't do

anything. They were called the Upfronts. I was singing, playing keyboards and writing songs. And when I was 17 I did my first arrangement for Rampart Records. I had lots of starving cold days but I really believed in my ability which kept me going. I worked free for a year and a half with a guy named Jack Stern who taught me how to produce sounds in the studio.

"I knew Bob Relf and Earl Nelson and I played keyboards on—and helped produce—their "Harlem Shuffle". And I did a thing with a guy named Leon Rene. And when Earl, he was Jackie Lee then, cut "The Duck" and it was a big hit, I went as his road manager. I gained a lot of experience.

"In 1966 I got the job of head of the A&R department for Mustang/Bronco Records who'd just been formed in Los Angeles. That was when I really found my purpose you could say. Writing and producing were like life to me. I did some things with Felice Taylor, Viola Wills and I sang a little bit myself. I had "All In The Run Of A Day", out on Bronco, but it kinda bombed. But Felice sold some, in fact "I Feel Love Comin' On" was a bigger success in Britain than here. She came to Britain but soon lost out.

"She was mechanical, a very mechanical singer. And she had a very bad attitude to the

business so she blew the whole thing.

"I left Mustang when it folded. What I had enjoyed most there was working with unknowns. I wasn't much interested in established artists. I just wanted to raise artists from the living dead. I knew that if I could find the right artist or group who'd allow me to implement the ideas in my head I could really set the world alight. In 1969 that happened. I found Love Unlimited.

"For two years I kinda groomed them. I'd recruited the girls, that's Diana Taylor, Linda James and Glodean James, from gospel music. We eventually all signed for Uni Records in 1971. I'd worked out this concept which involved a very complex production with rain effects, footsteps, a kinda story in sound. That was of course "Walkin' In The Rain With The One I Love" and of course it was very, very big. After that we put out their first album which sold pretty good.

"After a while the girls suffered a little while Uni label was folding and it took a while until we got them together of 20th Century. I'd signed with that company in the beginning of 1973. I'd never honestly thought too much about recording myself, I'd really lived for Love Unlimited. But when I cut "I'm Gonna Love You Just A Little Bit More Baby" I realised the public was willing to accept me as an

artist. Prior to that I made a duet with Jackie Lee. We called ourselves Smoke and had "Oh Love We Finally Made It" out on Mo Soul Records. But it was Love Unlimited who had the bigger seller with that song.

"Then I had my first album out on 20th Century and that went gold like "I'm Gonna Love You".

"The real superstars are the people who buy the records. Just imagine a million people getting together and agreeing on the same thing . . . that's something".

Since super-stardom Barry has cemented his firm financial base in the music world including a publisher Sa-Vette Music, a production company Soul Unlimited and Barry White Inc. But Barry is still happiest in the studio.

"I'm always trying for a very percussive sound. A lot of my sound comes from *being* personally involved with the production, the arrangement and the mix. Gene Page orchestrates but he writes what I tell him to write. I do the backing tracks before I put the vocals on. For an album it takes me two days of rhythm tracks, which means about eight sessions and after I get through with my rhythm and strings I bring in my voices, the girls or myself or another artist.

"Then I start mixing. I usually take an

hour and a half for each song, that's my limit.

"I've just finished working on a track by Love Unlimited. It's called People Of Tomorrow Who Are The Children Of Today. It's the closing song of a movie which I'm going to score for. The film is tentatively called "Mr. Cool" though the title could change. It's a mystery—a black cop gets killed and some black kids go out and find the killer. Writing for films has a lot of interest for me. But I refuse to write scores for dope pictures, Superfly kinda pictures. I'm anti-drugs, very much so.

"I've completed an instrumental album called "A Rhapsody In White". A lot of people have asked whether I was surprised that "Love's Theme" instrumental is a smash but I put so much work into each rhythm track I can understand the sound getting to the people. Love Unlimited will have a new album out shortly and I've begun putting down my own vocals for a new album. With new artists. I've done an album with Westwing. Also, I got a guy named Brock on 20th Century. I've also got an artist named Jay Dee on Warner Bros. which is terribly strong. Then there's a girl named Gloria Scott. And I'm working with a folk singer.

"You see I'm into *music*, not black music nor white music, Just Music."

# Maytals

**"Broadway Jungle" hit with a knock-out punch in 1967, an unstoppable ball of energy. And there were hundreds of other energy dancers who reacted in the same fashion whenever and wherever the record was played.**

It was a ska tune and the popular dance—the fast 'shuffle'—further ensured that there would be more than enough excitement around. As 'shuffling contests' broke out around the dance floor the dancers and onlookers would become even more excited, and that's when the fights would start. Looking back it seems that it was all part and parcel of the total energy that seemed to erupt whenever a great record like "Broadway Jungle" was played. "Broadway Jungle" or "Dog War" (as it was also known) introduced The Maytals to the dance floor of the Ram Jam club, South London.

Surely, through, I had heard this group before? I went and played "Six And Seven Books" and "Zachion" by The Vikings. Sure enough, The Maytals and The Vikings were one and the same band. The group had been singing for five years but I didn't jump on to their bandwagon until '67. From then on though I've been in the front seat and crowded as it is I ain't about to get out.

The Maytals are: Frederick Hibbert (Toots), Ralphus Gordon (Raleigh), and Nathaniel Matthias (Jerry). Jerry who is from Portland, Jamaica, was the first to start singing, he made his first record "Crazy Girl" for Duke Reid in 1958.

Toots is the youngest in the trip and in his family of eight—four brothers and three sisters—who all used to sing in church back in May Pen, Clarendon JA where he's from. It was a Baptist church, the lively, noisy type where everyone clapped their hands and sang their hearts out. Toots had to be placed on a box to praise the Lord, he was so small when he was younger. He left Clarendon in the fifties with his first guitar which he made himself, and stayed with a bigger brother in Kingston.

"I worked in a barber shop. I used to sing all the time and people would come around and listen and say I was good and I should go and record my voice. That's when I met Raleigh and Jerry. They came around and said they liked my singing and wanted to form a group. We sang together, rehearsing, and teaching each other. Then Raleigh came up which the name for the group—The Maytals."

They went to several promoters (producers or label owners, usually Sound System men) but none would give the trio a start. Toots says because his voice was too high then. In 1962 Coxon Dodd signed up The Maytals. Toots: "I already had the song 'Hallelujah' from when I was in Clarendon, it was a sort of spelling tune. We just got together

and worked out how to do it. It was nice to have a number one record, I just wanted to get another one."

Their next record "Fever" about a girl who gave the singer fever when he held her in his arms went to number one also. "Listen to me Raleigh" ("Toots!" comes the reply), "Listen to me Jerry ("Toots!"), "Please don't come too close or you'll caught, you'll caught, you'll caught my fever." Up to 1964 when The Maytals signed with Prince Buster all of their records were being issued by Coxon Dodd under the name of The Vikings. Although there was such a group they had no connection with The Maytals. "At that time the promoter didn't want people to know who really composed and sang the songs. Everywhere we went, people expected to see The Vikings instead of The Maytals and we lost a lot of money because of that."

The people who played on nearly all of The Maytals' ska records were always chosen from a clique of session musicians known as the "All Stars" and who for recording purposes later formed various permutations from their numbers and became known either as The Skatalites, or Baba Brooks' All Stars, or Roland Alphonso's All Stars, or Don Drummond And The Skatalites, etc. This pool of musicians were the following: Don Drummond and Reco Rodriguez (trombones), Roland Alphonso and Tommy McCook (tenor saxes), Lester Sterling and a guy called Hedley (alto saxes), Baba Brooks, Johnny Moore, and Raymond Harper (trumpets), Lloyd Nibbs alias "Drumbago" (drums), Lloyd Brevette and a guy called Blues (bass guitars), Jah Jerry (guitar), Jackie Mittoo (organ), Theophilous Beckford and Gladstone Anderson (pianos). These musicians contributed greatly to the success of many artists' records including The Maytals.

Many of The Maytals' biggest hit songs like "He Is Real", "Six And Seven Books" and "Zachion" and many more were overtly inspired by the church. Not only did they have the JA church gospel feel, the energy and spiritual flavour of the Baptist Church, but the lyrics were about biblical subjects like Zachion: "So come down Zachion come down, from off that sycamore tree." Toots: "If you have the love of God and know that it's God that will help you, then no matter what happens to you, you'll have the faith and the righteousness to overcome all troubles. I deal with love and righteousness and when you have that you just try to do things that are good, try to help who you can. That's why I sing in praise to God a lot of times. Some say Rastafari and Jah but they still go and do the wrong things so we just say righteousness and love."

Of course not all of their songs reflected these religious ideals. Songs like "Daddy" or "Domino" (about the most popular game in JA) endeared The Maytals to all sections of the community: "If you play six-five, I'll play six-four, I will look in my hand and double double–four / domino, *domino*, everybody likes domino." And "Daddy" has been re-recorded twice and each time it has been a chart topper throughout the Caribbean.

The Maytals left Coxon Dodd when their contract ended in 1964 immediately after "Six And Seven Book" was another number one hit. Sure enough all the promoters wanted the group but they still had the memory of the people who were so reluctant to give them an initial break. So they ignored many offers and signed a short term contract with Prince Buster.

With a popularity that was unequalled in JA and the Caribbean The Maytals were constantly in demand. There's something very special in a live Maytals' show, I've only seen them once but it's easy to imagine what their fans felt when after only being used to hearing the group's exciting records, they saw them on stage for the first time. For my own part I just automatically surrendered to the uncontrollable excitement that exuded from the three figures on the stage and seemed to envelop the lives of everyone in the audience—one life, one fate, one destiny. I could do nothing but sing and be devoured into the communal church—like atmosphere, it was church at its best—body and soul in praise! This is what The Maytals are really about, it's more than just music at its best, it's a religion, it's a fully fledged no holds barred Baptist meeting. Their music is about excitement, and peace and love, and goodness in God. As the song says "It was written down there—God is love".

In 1966 The Maytals entered the Jamaican Song Festival for the first time and won with "Bam Bam". By that time they were with a company called BMN along with manager Roy Nazrala and Byron Lee who handled their promotion. The group got to know Leslie Kong at that time too, because he also had an interest in the company. "When we won the Festival we received £600 and a lot of publicity and promotion on TV, radio, press, and we appeared at all the big theatres y'know! Byron Lee used to play with us, his group did the session for 'Bam Bam'."

Then came "Broadway Jungle", the record which epitomsed what the group was all about. The session musicians (The Skatalites) played typical hard driving ska. But it's the (call and response) staccato singing by Toots plus the scat shrieks by one voice and the other's regular rhythmic parts that create the real excitement. "Ska ba de ba day—'Hown' / Come on boy—'Hown' / Come on girl—'Hown' / Just *jump* into line—'Hown' / Rock your body in time—'Hown'." Toots: "I just started singing the song and the others added parts to it and we got that complicated sound so we called it 'Dog War' as well as 'Jamaica Ska' and they called it 'Broadway Jungle' in England."

The Maytals didn't enter the 1967 Festival but in '68 they came second with "Bim Today" and in '69 they won with "Sweet And Dandy". They missed the 1970 Festival, but were second with "Teacher Teacher" in 1971 and the last time they entered, they won with "Pomps And Pride" in 1972.

Every record The Maytals made in 1968 was outstanding. "54-46 That's My Number", "Struggle", "Just Tell Me", "We Shall Overcome", "Do The Reggay", "Hold On",

"School Days" and more. "Do The Reggay" was the first record to use the word reggay in the title and it really turned people on to the dance. But what became indicative of The Maytals' music was the number of what on the surface seemed to be protest songs. "We Shall Overcome" was such a song but Toots never intended "54-46" or "Struggle" as such.

Toots: "When I make a song I want you to think that what I sang about really happened or could happen. In fact '54-46'was my number in jail, but just like 'Jail House Rock' when they hear that a lot of people think that the singer went to jail and that's how he came to write the tune, but it's not. It just has to be written in a way that could be reality, a song must tell a story about something. Like in 'Struggle' a man is doing something that isn't good, so you tell him don't struggle because you'll get yourself in trouble. 'Struggle' is a song that I really used to like, it had good lyrics."

It was in 1968 also that The Maytals joined Leslie Kong, and they were with him up to 1970 when he died. And it was due to the talents of The Maytals, Jimmy Cliff, The Pioneers, etc. that Leslie Kong gained a reputation as a great producer. He did a lot of arranging for Desmond Dekker but people like Cliff, or The Maytals, did their own arranging and production musically. Toots told the session-men what to play, he played their instruments to them until they were able themselves to catch on and improvise.

"We always tried to make our sounds very different from anything else in Jamaica, to make them exclusive. In those times you had to keep the music moving. The reggae was just a new dance so we did 'Do The Reggay' but we mostly made faster tempo records anyway."

From 1968 to '70 The Maytals were the absolute tops in JA and in England, they still are but it's not quite so obvious now. Their first LP to be released in this country "Monkey Man" (Trojan TBL 107) contains possibly their best music—that is their most exciting, but "From The Roots" (Trojan TRLS 65), "Slatyam Stoot" (no longer available), and "Funky Kingston" (Dragon DRLS 5002) are all just as good really, the latter being the most polished and most soul flavoured. These albums contain the bulk of the best material from The Maytals since 1969 but there have been other great singles like "It's You", "Screwface Underground", "Walk With Love", "Watermelon Man", etc. plus the

more recent singles "Country Road" and "In The Dark".

Strangely but not surprisingly The Maytals have never had a top twenty record in this country. I'm sure they have sold hundreds of thousands of records to West Indians alone in England, but the media were never hip enough to be able to catch on to real talent when the time was right. And even the white English kids—the Skinheads—who were really into reggae music at one time seemed to bypass songs like "Pressure Drops" or "She's My Scorcher". They only ever picked up on "Bla Bla" and "Monkey Man" which I believe made the top fifty. And it was only after the JA movie "The Harder They Come" that the pop press picked up on The Maytals.

When Leslie Kong died The Maytals signed with Byron Lee and they're still with Dynamic Records. Their first single was "Redemption Song" another number one. Then came "It Was Written Down", another religious song. Toots: "Sometimes you have to take the time and sing in praise to the way of God, the Almighty must be pleased. So the lyrics come from your heart, deep down."

Songs like "Peeping Tom" (a song inspired when Toots caught someone 'peeping' on him), "Bla Bla" (one about a kind of jinx) and "Pressure Drops" were very popular with live audiences when The Maytals first went on tour in 1970. Nowadays The Maytals are always on tours and the audiences still request the older numbers but they expect to hear the more recent things like "Sit Right Down", "Pomps And Pride" and "Funky Kingston" in which Toots seems to be sounding more and more like Otis Redding.

"People tell me I sound like Otis Redding at times but I found that in myself a long time ago. I still appreciate it because he was a great singer anyhow!"

For over ten years The Maytals have been making uncountable hit records in Jamaica. No other group, no not even The Wailers have equalled their chart successes. But no one should be surprised that The Maytals aren't millionaires, no Jamaican musicians are.

Toots: "With all those hits we should have been earning much more money in all that time. But when you're young and you've just started, there's no one around to really help you get what you're entitled to. Everyone's trying to see how much they can make off you and you are just glad to be making a living. But I'm a professional now."

# John Holt

**John Holt sings middle-of-the-road pop songs. If he were white, and American, he'd probably be in the same bag as Jack Jones and earning as much money. But he's black and Jamaican, and he sings those songs in the idiom of his people, reggae. Maybe that's why he's still singing for peanuts.**

John's been singing for 12 years. He's 28 now, getting on a bit, but "never giving up" he says. He firmly believes that Jamaican music needs to be more 'commercial'. His last two LPs—"The Further You Look" and "1,000 Volts Of Holt"—with new manager Tony Ashfield, put it beyond doubt that he was headed in a pop direction. His LP "Dusty Roads" continues in that vein.

"Something's got to happen," he says, "but to really get this music on top, the artists, arrangers, and producers will have to add more instruments and of course write better songs."

It was become clear that reggae music will only be acceptable after it has been 'commercialised': it cannot succeed without being given a 'pop' treatment. "The Further You Look" LP was a best seller in Jamaican music last year because it was successful in doing this. For the first time horns, strings, flutes, and background vocals were added and arranged with imagination. The LP was easy to get into and hard to resist playing over and over again despite the not-so-happy theme of the lyrics.

But then John Holt has good reason to sing sad songs. The Jamaican music business does not usually produce happy musicians.

He sings specifically about love but his songs are not just products of his or others' relationships with women. They're not quite so narrow. Holt's hard life in the business, the frustrations and disappointments, are expressed in his songs despite being concealed by lyrics that only seem to deal with the love/emotions in a man-woman relationship.

He has a song out now called "Reggae In The Ghetto", untypically, of which he says: "A lot of people believe that reggae is coming from some sort of high society, so I'm explaining where it's really coming from. It was just a couple of local cats who got together and made this reggae thing, not some great orchestra or something." . . . Reggae is coming from the depths of the ghettos of Kingston, Jamaica. John is from Kingston, his love songs are from the ghettos too.

John Holt started singing for slices of cake at parties and wedding receptions. None of his four brothers and two sisters sings and his parents are devout Christians. But it wasn't the Church that discovered John's singing ability, it came out reluctantly at school.

"School really wasn't my thing . . . I preferred singing. I never attended a singing class though, I was scared. I was actually forced to sing in school by my friends, I didn't have the nerve y'know to really go out and do it."

In Kingston there were talent contests that catered for young aspiring singers. On Saturdays there was Lannaman's Children Hour, a recorded radio programme. Or there was Vere John's Hour. Other Opportunity Hours', as they were called, took place live at the local theatres or cinemas. John started singing the songs of Jimmy Clanton (his favourite singer) on these shows in 1960, competing with other would-be stars like Owen Gray, Jackie Edwards, Lascelles Perkins, Alton Ellis, and Jimmy Cliff.

"I used to whip Jimmy Cliff's bum y'know . . . he was afraid. If he knew I was gonna sing tonight for instance he wouldn't turn up."

When John won a final in 1962 his name and photograph appeared in the 'Star' and the 'Gleaner' (national newspapers) and about two days later promoter Leslie Kong appeared at John's door and asked him to make a record. "Forever I'll Stay"—an original composition—was a hit record but John didn't make any bread. So he got together with another fine singer, Alton Ellis, and made "Mouth A Massie Liza" and "Rum Bumper"—two big hits—for Randys Records. Still no bread. And after a short spell with Coxon Dodd's Studio One label John packed it in.

"Because things weren't so right, and you had better and bigger singers than myself like Owen Gray and Jackie Edwards. I was too far in the background so I quit for a while."

When John started singing again it was with a group called The Paragons which he formed with Bob Andy, Tyrone Evans and Howard Barrett in 1965. The Paragons went on to become one of the best and biggest groups in JA. Even though Bob Andy and John are both now solo performers the group is still active. In fact "Blackbirds Singing" was a big hit for them last year.

The Paragons' first hit "Love At Last" with promoter Coxon Dodd stayed at the top of the charts for five weeks. Other chart toppers included John's all-time favourite "Memories By The Score" plus "You're My Satisfaction" and "Love's Dream".

Bob Andy left the group in 1967 but stayed with Coxon Dodd as a solo singer having hits like "Too Experienced", "Games People Play" and others with Marcia Griffiths. Bob up to then had been the driving force of the band and when he quit, The Paragons suffered a temporary setback. However, with Holt's inspiration and guidance the group bounced back after about five months with strong chart topping material like "Only A Smile", "On The Beach", "Wear You To The Ball", "Happy Go Lucky Girl" and "Silverbird" on promoter Duke Reid's label.

The musicians on the Paragons' Duke Reid records were usually Tommy McCook and The Supersonics. But this group like many of those early ska/rock steady bands were no more than a studio band and did not have a rigid line-up. The Supersonics was just the name given to any set of musicians who happened to be on a particular session. Invariably these sessionmen came from a clique of close friends. They'd be described on the record label as The Supersonics, or The Skatalites, or Drumbago's All Stars and of course they were all the same group of musicians.

Nevertheless, the sounds did seem to take on different features and moods according to which band was supposed to be playing. Tommy McCook's Supersonics included Ernest Ranglin on guitar and Jackie Mittoo on organ, and their sound had a cool latin flavour

as opposed to The Skatalites' hard driving ska.

The Paragons' rock steady records were of a consistently high standard. In '67 especially—as the 'rock steady' caught on in England with West Indians—John Holt's warm, aching lead vocal rang out of the Sound System speakers and had you singing the pretty lyrics, and the heartbreaking choruses without knowing it. The Paragons of '67–'68 were a match for any group and John Holt was hot property. Pretty soon he was making solo records, not only for Duke Reid but for anyone who asked. Obviously he could no longer be restricted to the confines of The Paragons. He quit, but remained friends with the others.

Of Holt's early solo records, "Tonight", "I'm Your Man", "Ali Baba", "Do You Love Me For What I Am", "I'll Be Lonely" and "My Heart Is Gone" are best remembered. They were all very big hits. At one stage he had seven records in the charts.

Despite all this success artistically, there was no equivalent financial reward. Whether artists knew about royalties or not, they were never paid accordingly: they had to settle for small lump sums.

"You don't know where you stand as an artist in Jamaica. I didn't sing for any special promoter . . . just anyone who would pay me what I wanted. During those times and even now, it doesn't work out. If a cat even promises you royalties, you turn out getting crap instead! You don't get nothing. It's best to work for cash and get it over with one time. Otherwise you could wait over three months for royalties and get nothing but hard luck stories."

Many of the so-called 'producers' named on the record label never contributed to the actual construction of the music so in effect they were merely promoters. Of course there were very good individual producers (Holt himself has worked with Harry Moodie and Bunnie Lee for instance) but usually The Paragons worked out their own arrangements and did their own producing. So did John.

John Holt sings in a hard crooning style. His piercing tone echoes with melodrama even though the songs are not usually melodramatic, just plaintive. He sings lazily, unwilling to concede to the pace of the rhythm. Often he holds on to a note or syllable for longer than is necessary, seemingly reluctant to let it go. If this doesn't hook you then his graceful, aching tenor on songs like "My Heart Is Gone" or "I'll Always Love You" surely will. The listener is made to believe that these songs are the result of some true and harsh experiences.

This is why The Paragons were one of the heroes of rock steady music, a music which was itself spiritually uplifting. You could lose yourself in the pulse of the music and discover yourself singing and/or dancing uncontrollably. No wonder when U. Roy started using The Paragons' records in 1970 as the background music for his overdubbed shouted phrases (dj music). It wasn't long before U. Roy became a star in his own right. His success was built on the music of The Paragons and specifically John Holt who composed, arranged, and sang lead. Inevitably U. Roy ran out of steam when there were no more Paragons' songs left to use.

"Really and truly," says John, "I think that the dj records were one of the things that lowered the standard of Jamaican music. These artists are trying to sing now."

After exhausting the theatres and clubs in Jamaica, where top artists can appear, John came to England for the first time in 1968. But his stage debut here wasn't made until 1970 at the Wembley Reggae Festival. The first solo LP available in this country was released by Junior Lincoln's Bamboo Records and included material like "Tonight" and "A Love I Can Feel" (the title track) which had helped him to win awards as the 'best male vocalist' that year (a title he also held for the next two years).

Then came the albums "Still In Chains",

"Holt" and "Pledging My Love", all produced by Bunnie Lee—a man known for getting results in Jamaica. They are all good LPs, the best being the latter due to the greater percentage of very good material. "Chains" has at least one very outstanding cut in "Just Out Of Reach", similarly "Holt" contains the fabulous "Stick By Me" (John's biggest seller), but "Pledging My Love", which includes one Ray Charles and three Johnny Ace songs, has a more consistent mood than the other two.

The most outstanding of his own compositions "I'll Always Love You" reappeared on John Holt's next, and arguably best album so far "The Further You Look" (Sings For I'). When it first appeared, there was initial disappointment at the obvious search for 'commerciality'. The rhythms seemed too far in the background, there were sweet lilting strings, horn, flutes, and background vocals. John's voice seemed less emotional. Gradually, though, his vocals shone through and the rest of the music followed. The LP sold like hotcakes in the West Indian community. After a year it's still selling well, it still sounds as good.

The change in style was brought about by John's manager, an Englishman named Tony Ashfield who used to run a Sound System. Tony went into record production with the owner of a small studio, Terry Newman (John's road manager) when they met in 1968. Tony, a JA music fanatic, reckoned that John Holt was the best singer. John was introduced to Tony by a mutual friend and the two decided to work on "The Further You Look" in December '70. The rhythms as always were recorded under John's supervision at Dynamic Studio in JA. Everything else was done in England at Intersound and Lansdowne Studios with help from string arranger Brian Rogers, who will also conduct the orchestra when John performs on stage. His latest album, "1000 Volts Of Holt", shot to the top of the British reggae charts on release proving that the people liked the pop-styled John Holt.

"What we're trying to do is to build up an English standard to see if it can make the charts. Instead of just having raw rhythms, Tony Ashfield got Brian Rogers to do some string, horn, and flute arrangements. I would hope that these records get some airplay. I'll never stop singing until I make the British charts. I would really love to swing with reggae and to see it swing, because it's our thing, Jamaica's thing. It's no Johnny Nash thing.

"I would ask these BBC djs to listen to a few good Jamaican songs, not just mine, and voice a fair opinion. But I criticise the Jamaican radio stations for playing so many English and American records. It's as if they don't want any Jamaican artists to get rich, that's what I really think! Y'see they don't want artists to have as good or an even better standard of living than themselves, so they play foreigners' records, it's really true! They don't want Jamaican artists to outdo them.

"But Tony Ashfield and myself will always try to make the reggae thing better. I only hope that God will speak in these djs hearts and make them play some good reggae."

# Isley Bros

**SURELY those three vaguely seedy-looking guys in greasy processes and slick mohair suits who sang "Twist And Shout" 11 years ago can't be the same cool dudes who are currently giving out with the super-70s wah-wah funk on "That Lady"?**

You better believe it. The Isley Brothers have come a long way, and their 15-year career has involved them with most of the biggest record labels, most of the top producers and many of the top musicians (including Jimi Hendrix—but more of that later). It's also brought them four million-sellers.

No, they aren't a product of the seventies . . . nor even the sixties. And Kelly Isley (he dropped the 'O' from O'Kelly) patiently related a history of extraordinary dues paying . . .

Mama Isley was a God-fearing woman who sang her belief to anyone who'd listen and she brought her numerous children up the same way. Four of her kids sang, accompanied by Mom on creaking church pianos, in auditoriums all over Ohio, though mainly their hometown of Cincinnati. She needed her faith when one of her sons was run over and killed by a truck. The remaining three, Rudolph, Ronald and O'Kelly were ready to quit on their brother's death. Somehow they got over the shock and sang on.

In the fifties the uplifted scream-of-joy of gospel music rubbed shoulders with the introvert moan of anguish of the blues, cool doo-wop harmony exercises and the raunchy, boogying bit beat in the black pop music mainstream. Clyde McPhatter, the Five Royales and the Dominoes in the fifties paved the way for Top 40 testifying in the sixties—the sound of soul.

The three raw teenagers decided to 'cross the secular line' and chase pay dirt. So when Ronald hit 16 the Isleys climbed on a bus to New York. The year was 1957.

On the bus they met a lady called Beelah Bryant—it was their first break.

"Beelah Bryant began to call different agents and different record companies and make appointments for us to meet people to see if they could do anything for us. Sure enough she got several record companies pretty interested and she called up a guy by the name of Nat Nezerro who at that time managed Pearl Bailey and Step'n Fetchit and we sung to this guy over the phone. You know he thought we were jivin' him by playing a record or somethin'. So he asked us to come over to his office. We did and he dug.

"Within two weeks we did our first engagement in Washington D.C. at the Howard Theatre and we made more money than we'd ever made in our life. They gave us $550 for the week and from the Howard Theatre we went to the RKO Palace on Broadway—that's where they had all the vaudeville shows. So the next week we did the Apollo Theatre. We would take-off the Patti Page tune 'Rock and Roll Waltz' and we closed with Frankie Lymon & The Teenagers' number 'Why Do Fools Fall In Love'.

"We started getting even more—RKO's was $750 then at the Apollo we got $950. Then we met a guy who owned a record company called Teenage Records—we signed a contract and made our first recording, it was called 'The Angels Cried'. We saw it break out in Cincinnati and we thought *fantastic* but it sold nothing to brag about. But we *could* brag it was our first recording. Teenage Records were in New York.

"After the record wasn't as big as we thought it could have been we wanted a release from Teenage Records and the guy wouldn't give us a release—he said he had a contract on us. He didn't have a contract . . . although we'd signed one. He left the contract on his desk after the signing and we picked it up—he must have thought he had it in his file. I imagine he tore his whole office apart looking for his contract. So we were free and clear to go with anyone we wanted to. That was George Goldner—Gone Records."

It was 1959 when they went to the king of the New York vocal group hustlers, George Goldner. George couldn't go wrong with the Teenagers, Imperials, Flamingos and countless others. Doo-wops just weren't the Isley's forté, nor for that matter was knock-'em-down rock 'n roll. But George tried the brothers with a bit of each. Neither doo-wops ("My Love") nor rock ("Rockin' McDonald") sold, though the 'formula' was the same as Goldner's hits.

"We recorded several records. They had a funny way of recording back in those days . . . the studios were working the full 24 hours and they would bring in maybe ten groups and record enough tunes for dozens of discs. Richard Barrett did the productions and Dave Cortez played piano."

After four singles with Goldner (one on Cindy, one on Mark-X, and two on Gone) they drifted into another recording contract. But this was *the big one*.

Hugo Peretti knew how to produce hits and he, and partner Luigi were scoring a plenty with RCA. Hugo knew less about making black music than he did about making dollars, so after signing the Isleys who had come into their offices with a dub of one of their Gone sides, he tried them with a slice of coy banality "I'm Gonna Knock On Your Door". It didn't sell vast amounts and vast amounts of sales were what RCA wanted.

"Now we were doing a show at Washington D.C. and singing a big tune which had been recorded by Jackie Wilson called 'Lonely Teardrops' and we sang this song and we got to the end and just started to adlib and Rudolph was playing to the audience who were jumping up and shouting and stuff so Rudolph starts a wailing' 'get your hands up and get your feet up and shout!' everybody shout! So later we said 'say why don't we write a song like that' . . . and so we wrote 'Shout'."

On the 29th July 1959 the classic "Shout" Pts. 1 & 2 was recorded. It sounds wild today, in 1959 it sounded positively demented. Nothing as commitedly, emotionally, black had been put out on RCA, and it was with undisguised surprise that the RCA execs' saw it rise up to hot 100. White as well as black kids caught the excitement. It made 47 before sliding out again and subsequently became a standard catalogue 'golden oldie' generating enough sales for a return to the charts in '62 and an eventual millionth sale.

But how do you follow "Shout"? They next put on wax a song written a couple of years previously "Respectable". It didn't make charts but sold so, so. But where "Shout" was all guts and fire, "Respectable" was all catchiness and bounce even though Ronald's raucous lead gave it a certain clipped excitement.

Their first album "Shout" was released in 1960 and straddled as many musical barriers as you'd expect from RCA's something-for-everybody policy. On 'St. Louis Blues' and 'That Lucky Old Sun' the group tried to breathe fiery life into creaking material. But the picture of the group dressed in baggy white suits leaping in the air caught a little of the atmosphere of a wild act which included splits, cartwheels and heart attacks for the easily shocked.

Peretti couldn't get it together with the group again and after a dismal failure with "Gypsy Love Song", RCA tried fellow staffer Sammy Lowe to produce a hit. But strings and choirs killed any chance of chart action. "When we went to RCA the people we dealt with were old men of 50 or 60 or even 70. They couldn't understand any of the acts." So they moved to Atlantic.

Atlantic Records had driven inroads down chittlin street since the late forties and therefore should have known what to do with wild gospel screamers. But they first put them with the Ray Ellis Orch. for a disc "Teach Me To Shimmy". It was wild enough, but corny as well. It bombed. Leiber & Stoller were sent for and although they produced some fine, fine, music ("Write To Me" a gentle lilter and "A Fool For You" a no-holds-barred preacher from the Ray Charles Songbook) three discs went nowhere. The time was set for them to change again.

Florence Greenberg was a strange autocratic lady who ran a record label like she was the artists' personal benefactor. Her labels Wand & Scepter were establishing themselves with hits. She was using as staff producer Bert Berns who was beginning to etch a unique place for himself in the producers' heavenly hall of fame by fusing Spanish instrumentations and arrangements into black music to evolve "Black Latin Soul". After a flop with "Right Now" a churchy wailer a new session was booked for the boys.

"We spent most of a session recording a Burt Bacharach tune 'Make It Easy On Yourself'. At the end of the session we did one take of 'Twist And Shout'. What happened was that Burt Bacharach wanted to change the words of the tune, so 'cause of that our version wasn't released. 'Twist And Shout' was of course."

"T & S" was written by Bert Berns and Phil Medley a year previously and given to Atlantic who put out the Top Notes doing it . . . fairly nondescriptly. The song of course: "Twist And Shout".

Chubby Checker's "The Twist" had recently dropped from No. 1 (where it had been for the second time) when in early 1962 the trio and a bunch of Teacho Wiltshire directed session men cut "Twist and Shout" for a nation ecstatic with the new giration. Not that "Twist And Shout" was good to twist to . . . it's beat was too fast and too fierce . . . but with the Russell cocktail of fierce "La Bamba" rhythms on electric guitars mixed with hell-for-leather screaming by Rudolph its appeal was instant. It got to 17 in Billboard's pop charts and stayed a hit for 16 weeks selling a million and giving the group a new itinerary of club and theatre dates.

The Isley Brothers *were* excitement and with the early sixties sound of pop an emasculated plastic one the brothers' style was welcomed by whites and blacks alike. "Twist And Shout" sold nothing in Britain of course, that is 'til four Liverpudlians grated through the number on their first album and focused a new interest in the song and its hit recordists . . . but that comes later.

The groups followup "Twistin' With Linda" has none of the magic of "T & S" in fact its "Around and around and around" chanting was strict Cameo-Parkway tradition though a screaming climax at least gave it some guts. It was a smallish hit but the hits stopped for them and Wand, even though "Nobody But Me" was a fine example of uncontrolled freneticism. The "Twist And

Shout" album was a peculiar pastiche of good and bad, froth-at-the-mouth excitement and laboured quasi-latinesque. And once again the group moved labels.

United Artists records tried hard to record interesting productions and "She's Gone", a sobbing soul dirge originally written for Ben E. King and recorded by the Isleys after Ben rejected it—neurotic lyrics cried over a Spectorian accompaniment—and interesting songs ("Who's That Lady" the original version of their T-Neck smash) and then put them on flip sides of discs they didn't promote. Also an album of mainly R&B standards and a bizarre "Surf And Shout" soon landed in the discount bins of a thousand record stores.

But the Isleys still had a reputation as major 'on stage' performers even boosted by the Beatles raving in the press about their discs. So the Isleys thanked the Fab Four . . . on record. It was 1964 when the group first formed a label called T-Neck, named after Teaneck, New Jersey, where they lived. By this time their band included an unknown, skeleton-thin guitarist called Jimi Hendrix. T-Neck's one release, distributed by Atlantic, didn't sell . . . which is a shame as although the song "Testify" with a series of references to artists like Jackie Wilson, Stevie Wonder and the Beatles ("Right *now* they got some soul!" screams Rudolph) was pretty muddled it came complete with Hendrix and a screaming guitar solo and was wild enough to go for your throat.

"With T-Neck what happened was Jerry Wexler said, we would get the records distributed better and faster if they were on the Atlantic label and not T-Neck. So after "Testify" they put the others on Atlantic saying 'A T-Neck Production'."

When they switched to Atlantic they tried the four S's—sophisticated sweet soul sound. "The Last Girl" an Isley composition, a beautiful ballad, *nearly* made it. Wasn't that a harp with the lush strings and how did Jimi Hendrix manage to get on this session? But Atlantic's followup "Simon Says" disappointed, sing-a-longy stuff, neither sweet nor particularly soulful. Papa Gordy was ready to take them in hand. Motown Records were making so many hits by the mid-sixties that lesser corporations would have been punch drunk. When Motown signed the Isleys hits were expected, even if some were surprised as the wild gospelly histrionics appeared to run at cross purposes to the sophisticated 'sound of young America'.

Motown's dividend reapers needn't have worried. The Isleys were placed with Holland, Dozier & Holland who had only to scratch their bums to make Top 20. So the group became part of a larger family and had hits again: "This Old Heart Of Mine" (No. 12), "Take Some Time Out For Love" (No. 66), "I Guess I'll Always Love You" (No. 61). The "This Old Heart Of Mine" album is a milestone and as instantly catchy as measles. It bubbles and bounces joyfully and although some, me included, regretted the compromise of gospel passion to Four Topsey whimsey, the effect was still devastating—the productions were masterpieces of rhythm, melody and soul . . . glossy version of course. But all was not well.

"I remember one time we went to the Copacabana to see the Supremes and Berry Gordy Jr. was there and came up and said "Hey! How you doing? Congratulations—"This Old Heart Of Mine" is a smash and everything but everyone in the company's mad with me you know." So we said "What for?" So he says "You're new at Motown and you've got a smash hit but some of our artists have been with us years you know. They don't dig you getting the best material. We thought he was joking—we found out he wasn't."

When the good songs stopped coming so did the hits. And with HDH leaving Motown in a flurry of law suits the Isley's, after some stereotyped Motown factory singles with other producers, left Big Brother with a disgruntled rejection of mohair suits. West Coast groups, flower power, mind expansion, youth revolution—the late-sixties were changing times and change was a comin' for the Isleys. For more than a decade they had been the tools, willing or unwilling, of production super giants; Hugh & Luigi, Bert Berns, Leiber & Stoller, Holland-Dozier-Holland, and now *they* decided to wield the hammer of production. T-Neck, a failed enterprise of yesteryear, was resurrected—gloriously.

"Times had changed you know. We had like years of experience with that many companies that we had bound to have picked up some knowledge so we used it . . ." "It's Your Thing" the first of the 'new' Isleys was a hit, a smash, a blockbuster. It's millionth sale brought bookers hungrily calling for the group's appearances in a thousand clubs and theatres. They were no doubt surprised by the publicity pics of the group scowling militantly and dressed in African robes and appalled that the group was no longer prepared to work for peanuts. Monkeys they were not. The strident fusion of dance rhythms of "Thing" make it a dance classic, wah-wah funk before people had figured out soul could be 'progressive' and with a simple lyric which helped maintain mounting awareness of blackness, sexual preference, youth or any other "thing". 1969 was a good year: "I Turned You On" ("I turned you on and I can't turn you off"), "Black Berries" ("the blacker the berry the sweeter the juice"), "Was It Good To You" ("I wanna know was it good to ya!") all had the sexuality of the lyric emphasised by the sensuality of the rhythm accompaniment.

The brothers had been joined by two more of their family: Ernie (guitar), Marvin (bass) together with organist fantastique 'Dave Baby' Cortez and later keyboard man Chris Jasper—now an officially adopted Isley insured a hypnotic range of funk behind searing, extrovert vocals—the group had come of age. Their songs were mostly originals "Get Into Something", "Warpath" and "If He Can You Can" occasionally slipping in a 'rock' standard (Steve Stills "Love the one You're With" or Dylan's "Lay Lady Lay") and, on each, behind Rudolph's wailing exuberance there's a rhythm track put down by some of the first black heavy metal kids.

T-Neck thrived and although the only strong seller outside of the Brothers Three (a pseudonym they used for their "Turn On, Tune In, Drop Out" single and as the title to one of their T-Neck funk power albums) was the Vandals' "In My Opinion" (lead vocalist Damon Harris now an established Temptation) they kept their distributing company Buddah more than happy.

In 1971 they laid 400,000 dollars on the table to produce a feature film documentary of a soul concert. The film "It's Your Thing" starred the Isleys with the 5 Stairsteps, Moss Mabley, Ike & Tina and assorted soul artists big and small. It crawled on release in Britain and although Paramount distributed, reaction was somewhat lukewarm.

A couple of disc flops provoked the Brothers to look around for a new set-up to bring their goodies into every shop in the land. In mid 1973 Columbia Record Corporation—high on the crest of the Philly soul wave—brought yet new direction and fresh greenbacks to the group. "That Lady" their first 'Columbia T-Neck' notched up two million sales. And the album '3 + 3' (available here on CBS) was yet a new direction:—hard and aggressive, sweet and mellow, all defiantly modern . . . and eclectic.

"Columbia has to be the biggest thing ever to get our kind of music to the people . . . Our music is changing, our experience is widening and so is our audience. We can be real heavy, we can be sweet, we can be down home and soulful."

The huge, mass audience they will now reach is ready for their changes. And after so many years of sweat ain't that justice?

Isleys through the Ages

# Harold Melvin

**"THE success we have now obtained is beautiful. But I don't think anyone can say that success came easy."**

Lawrence Brown, member of Harold Melvin And The Bluenotes, spoke thoughtfully. It was 10 o'clock on a Monday morning in a Los Angeles hotel room. The group had gigged the night before and Lawrence's voice was thick through lack of sleep. Yet sleeplessness did not blur his memory.

"We started way, way back in 1954. We were just a bunch of schoolkids then. The group was myself—and I was only 11, a kid called Frankie who was our first lead singer, Harold Melvin, Bernard Wilson and a guy we called Brodie. We called ourselves the Bluenotes. In 1956 we plucked up enough courage to try for a recording audition. We went to Josie Records who were hitting with the Cadillacs. They had good distribution and we thought a record with them would be a big deal. We recorded "If You Love Me". You know, the standard . . . 'If the sea should suddenly run dry' . . . It sold some locally and we started doing record hops and the odd rock and roll show. But Josie just didn't get behind us and we never saw much bread.

"We soon realised that we weren't gonna get too far in the chittlin' circuit—you know small black clubs for ten dollars a night—so we tried to develop a night club act. We learnt Broadway tunes, got some fancy clothes and tried to get into the white night club thing. It wasn't easy but we managed, and by 1960 we were doing OK despite having no records on the market. Brodie had left by then.

"In '60 we eventually were able to leave Josie and went to a guy who was like a forerunner of Berry Gordy—a black record label owner. That was Doc Bagby. He was a pretty big band leader in the fifties. He started a company called Value Records and we did a song with him called "My Hero". It was a reasonable hit (78 in the Hot 100, October 1960). We played the Apollo then. But the followup, called "Hot Chills Cold Thrills and Fever" didn't sell and Value were running into difficulties. Again, we had to fall back on club work. Our lead left to get married and we got in a new group member John Atkins. Harold Melvin took over as the main lead, though it was shared quite a bit. We needed to make more money. Harold felt there had to be another way to go."

That way was shown to them in the early sixties by Martha Reeves whose Vandellas were well on the way to making Motown a million bucks. Martha knew that the chittlin' circuit, or even the smaller white clubs, wouldn't get a group out of the no-bread

situation and she introduced the Bluenotes to some big timers in the William Morris Agency. By now the group were considerably more than 'another group' and had enough confidence and flexibility to turn in a passable 'nightclub' act. They wore tails and bow ties, sang the hits of the shows, and playing safe with the middleaged whites in Las Vegas, Lake Tahoe, Puerto Rico, and Miami. They began to see real paydirt.

In 1964 the group (credited for the first time as Harold Melvin and the Bluenotes) recorded for Landa records. "Get Out" sold a few (125 in the pop charts) but its indistinct vocal approach, part doo-wop part soul, left little impression of the group's capability. So club work continued.

"In the mid-sixties we were working in Philadelphia and Richard Barrett heard us. He'd just finished with Swan Records and had started his own company. We cut a couple of songs with him but the record didn't sell. After that in 1967 were doing a gig in a Miami nightclub when Luther Dixon saw us. Luther was a kinda legend with all those hit songs and productions for Scepter records.

"He took us into the Criterion Studios and we cut some sides: "Goodbye My Lover Goodbye", "I Can't Take My Eyes Off You"—the Franki Valli song and some other things. They released a single on Chess.

"None of those sides sold a lot though we used to sell 500 a week ourselves at the clubs we were playing! A year or so later we cut our first album. It was the kind of material we were doing in our nightclub act, some Broadway tunes—our first recording of "Cabaret"—some Temptations songs, a bit of everything. It wasn't actually recorded live though it was put out with that hype. We did that for Charlie Stone. Again we sold it mostly ourselves in the clubs, we had to handle our own distribution!"

In 1970 they tried a recording session in Miami with the Alston/Glades label group.

The Harold Melvin penned "Never Gonna Leave You" (released on the Dash label) had it moments but the generally reliable Steve Alaimo and Willie Clark turned in a messy production job. They needed a new production approach if they were going to get a big record. They found it in their home town with two old school buddies, but first the group had to get itself sorted out.

"When we were on the road—which was just about permanently—we always had our own backing band, maybe five or six instruments. Around '59 we heard our drummer Theodore Pendergrass sing something and we thought 'there's a voice the Bluenotes need'. Theodore has a very hoarse, soulful voice. In '70 the group broke up for a while—there were disagreements about what we should be doing and where we should be going—and when we reformed after a few months John Atkins, who'd been taking on more and more of the lead work left and Theodore joined the Bluenotes. So that's when we got our final line-up. Harold Melvin, Theodore 'Teddy' Pendergrass, Lloyd Parkes—he joined us about '69, Bernard Wilson and myself."

Teddy Pendergrass, with a rough-edged, abrasive vocal style, similar in tone to the Dell's Marvin Junior, had started in soul music young. He worked for a while as drummer-come-singer with the James Brown Review. Lloyd Parkes sang previously in a Philly group, the Epsilons who had a superb, though small selling disc "The Echo" on Stax in the late sixties.

"When Kenny (Gamble) and Leon (Huff) had first approached us about recording in the sixties we hadn't been very keen. You see then we didn't have a very serious attitude towards recording. Like sure we'd record a side here and there but club work was how we *ate*, like working with Kenny and Leon would mean a month with no pay so to speak! But we rapped and came to the decision that

things were gonna change for the Bluenotes. I mean up until then we'd been trying to be a whole group of Sammy Davis Jr's—we'd not been selling records, well not to the kids. But we knew that with Theodore doing that soulful lead and Kenny and Leon allowing us the freedom to express ourselves we could make it. In 1972 we signed with Philadelphia International."

The formula for Kenny and Leon's success owed a lot to inspired originality and a little to Chicagoan Bobby Miller who with the Dells had evolved putting a very raw, emotionally soulful voice and sweet harmony backup with large, near-symphony orchestras and thundering dramatic rhythm lines. Gamble and Huff's development of this idea struck gold, or near to it, right off. In 1972 a meandering two-part soul ballad "I Miss You" smashed into first the soul and then the pop charts.

"On "I Miss You" Theodore sang the lead, Lloyd did falsetto, Harold the monologue and we all backed up! Our two Gamble/Huff albums have made it for us of course. Our second single "If You Don't Know Me By Now" got us a platinum record—two million sales—though our third "Yesterday I Had The Blues" wasn't that big. Looking back on the first album, it was called "I Miss You" then changed to "Harold Melvin And The Bluenotes" we're all pretty proud of it, it's a very *soulful* soul album. But I believe "Black And Blue" is stronger. The first single from that, "The Love I Lost", was a smash of course. You know it's funny how Leon and Earl (Young) only found that uptempo shuffle rhythm by accident, when we started rehearsing it was a ballad. On "Black And Blue" we do "Cabaret", Basiestyle, but there's some real heavy soul as well.

"We owe a lot to Gamble, Huff, all the Philly session men—yeah, they're the *greatest*—but after these years in the business we owed success to ourselves too."

Harold Melvin and the Bluenotes

Barry White

Black Music Gallery

Smokey Robinson
pre-solo days with
The Miracles

# Smokey Robinson

**"I don't think there's such a thing as reaching the top in music, that you can get to the summit and say 'hey, I've reached the heights of music'. That's impossible as far as I'm concerned. There are always new ideas, new lyrics, new melodies."**

It was with warm relief that we discovered that Smokey's new lyrics, new melodies, have the same magic as his old. When we had all recovered from the thought of a Miracles without a Smokey it seemed a long time to wait for that first solo album from the man Bob Dylan called the 20th Century's greatest poet and who still makes a sweet song of romantic love appear plausible even in such cynical times. Smokey sounded as warm as his songs when he talked about his solo LP and his personal philosophy apparent within the microgroove.

"I don't think I'm a romantic . . . just a person who loves love . . . I wish there was more of it in the world."

The album "Smokey" is a fine record. "Baby Come Close": (Let me touch your heart, let the fire start, Ooh so warm, so warm") has a honey-coated vocal which glides with effortless beauty. Love is still the centre of the world which Smokey sings about. And when you lose love? Well, Smokey can put new poignancy, new meaning, into Carole King's "Will You Love Me Tomorrow". But Smokey realises that a voice of such sensual depth shouldn't sing just of love, its gain, its loss. In recent years Curtis Mayfield, Marvin Gaye and Donny Hathaway have all sung of loveless society: poverty, violence intolerance, injustice. And now, so does Smokey.

"The initial music for "Just My Soul Responding" was done by a guy who has been with me since my time with the Miracles, he's still with me in fact, Mr. Marv Tarplin. We've done many songs together, "Tracks Of My Tears", "My Girl Is Gone" different tunes like that. We're here in California writing together now. 'Just My Soul Responding' was inspired by his music. Those words are of course a lyric which deals with *the* problem of the country that I live in today—the huge injustice in the treatment of the Red Indian. The Sioux medicine chant is done by Tom Bee. Tom's a Navajho Indian and he is in a group who we formerly had here called XIT. He did the chant for me because I wanted it to be authentic and I wanted it to really mean what the lyric was saying about the depressive situation of the American Indian living here, having been pushed into a reservation in a land that once *belonged* to him. Like if you go home tonight and somebody's in your place and they say 'O.K. now you can live in this one room in the back of your house . . . and don't come out.' Now that's the same kinda thing. And *that's* the reason why I did that song. Also, of course, the last verse of "Just My Soul Responding" deals with the black man's situation."

The album has a piece of vintage Smokey story-in-song, "A Silent Partner In A Three Way Love Affair". Only Smokey could draw such a succinct picture of the pain of a triangle of interwoven relationships.

"How do I write a song? Well, that's a question that has about 2,000 answers because there is no actual way, there's no actual formula. As far as I'm concerned. I believe in God and I believe he sent me a message to do this—the melody, the words. I might be in the tub and the melody might come. I might be driving in my car and some words might come. There are a lot of songs I write which I never record. But I don't necessarily feel I am recording the cream of my compositions. Some of them I record on other people but I don't cut them myself, and then some of them I might write and they're just there, they're just stored away, not necessarily because they're bad songs or something. Then there are some I write that I think are horrible so I throw them away or I keep because they have one good idea in them that perhaps I can spin off and get an idea for another song which would be better than the number I'd originally written."

At times the arrangements on "Smokey" are slightly over-lush but the general feel of the production is as crisp as a new carrot. Listen to the fine rhythm section, the light and shade of eclectic, sophisticated orchestrations. Willie Hutch—the co-producer with Smokey—has done a fine job in fusing funk, flair and finesse.

"Willie Hutch is definitely going to be a very big name in music before his time is up. He's definitely a very talented young man, he's really involved in his music. He's done a lot of things around here with Motown, however he'd just got off the ground when he did the soundtrack for "The Mack". I really dig working with him.

"The album took a long while to record simply because of the fact that I was taking my time. I could have finished it up sooner, but I wasn't rushing on any of the songs, I wasn't anxious to finish it or anything like that. And I would say for the first time in my career of recording that it was just me, I didn't have to worry about what's going to happen to this guy over here if I don't hurry up and record it. Whatever happens, it's all me so I should take my time and do it. July of 1972 was when I left the Miracles. That's been quite a while as far as I'm concerned. However, I still have a very close-knit relationship with the Miracles and I see them very often and we're still tied-up family-wise. It's really a beautiful thing because the guy they have now who's singing in my place is a beautiful person and he's gonna do great things with them I'm sure."

Does Smokey solo differ that much from those nostalgic days of Miracles? Not really. There's still the lilt of wistful melody, the occasional upsurge of gut-feeling, still Claudette singing those sweet backups with her distinctive little voice—as memorable as any solo artist's. "Recording my wife solo is my next project. I don't know whether I'm gonna do a complete LP at first but I'm certainly going to get into recording stuff on her for a couple of singles, which I hope will lead to an album."

In all, "Smokey" is an album to play and cherish. We can only hope that such fine things can be forthcoming on his next one.

"I didn't necessarily feel I should immediately do it—but I have started to work on new tunes, which are gonna be a new album and I'm hoping that it's gonna be good, that's

no ad

all I can do—work on it, hope it turns out for the best."

But its not only records that Smokey now wishes to involve his talents in.

"I do feel that I'd like to do everything in connection with films one day. I'd probably like to act in some, do scores, maybe even produce and direct some one day. A few years back I composed the title tune for the "Come Spy With Me" movie, which was probably the worst movie ever made, but that was at a time when we had never had anybody from our organisation doing music for movies. And so when we were approached, due to enthusiasm, and not knowing what the film was going to be about, or who was going to be in it, or anything of that type, we agreed to do the title tune. We flunked it and I think it was the worst movie ever."

But Smokey knows celluloid stardom can only be so many frames of a shutter away. Not that stardom, riches, nor ego, matter much to the man who sings about good things, of love and humanity.

"You never rise above humanity. I don't care what you do in life, what material things you gain, or what status you gain in life, you're still a human being. You were born and you're gonna die, you get sick and you have fun and you're sad. Everybody does the same things. You can never rise above that."

# Stylistics

**Airron Love, spokesman for the Stylistics, didn't seem to realise he was announcing something guaranteed to reduce thousands of the group's loyal following to hand-wringing grief.**

"We've just cut an album without Thom Bell. Our producers on that are Hugo and Luigi. The songs and arrangements will be Van McCoy's. You see at the time we were booked to go back into the studio to cut an LP, Thom (Bell) was fully tied-up with other sessions until June. So we went and recorded without him."

Critics might be tempted to observe that recording the Stylistics without Thom Bell is like designing a motor car without wheels. But if you believe that the heart-fluttering falsetto of Russell Thompkins Jr., and the smooth as silk, sensual harmony of his fellow Stylistics, is as essential an ingredient to the Stylistics' gold disc brew as the lush, plush and deft productions and mind-capturing songs of maestro Mr. Bell, fear not. A plunge into the sea of mediocrity seems as unlikely as Airron's sincerity in talking about Thom Bell seems certain.

"Obviously, we owe Thom a great, great deal. And equally obviously, we want to record with Thom again. I'm sure we'll get together again. He's taken us a long way since our first record."

Yet the Stylistics first record was without Thom Bell—without any super-stereo sophistication of production and arrangement—and still sold enough to start the vocal team on the hit road therefore bypassing the usual years of shuffling along the backstreets of obscure recording contracts and no money gigs. Those kind of deals were more the kind of trips of the Stylistics forerunners—the Monarchs and the Percussions. In 1965 both groups were formed in Philadelphia. Philly had been one of the centres of the fifties doo-wop boom, but it was now attempting to shrug off the embarrassing memory of Dick Clark's Bandstand and Bobby Rydell, Chubby Checker and a sea of banality which threatened to drown rock and roll. Soul Music came to the rescue.

Not that the Monarchs nor the Percussions contributed much. For three years they played the tiny clubs before disbanding. But a hybrid sprang up. From the Monarchs came Russell Thompkins Jr., Airron Love and James Smith and from the Percussions—Herbie Murrell and James Dunn. The new group dubbed

James Brown

Dandy Livingstone

themselves the Stylistics. Things looked up a bit. The Stylistics toured Pennsylvania with a backing quintet (now expanded to six) Slim & The Boys. In 1969 the guitarist with the Boys, Robert Douglas wrote, with the Stylistics road manager Morty Bryant, a song which belonged more in the age of baggy panted doowopers than the sixties sounds of soul. They gave it to the Stylistics . . . to record.

"We cut "You're A Big Girl Now" for a guy called Bill Perry. Bill ran a label called Sebring Records. It was our first record but we weren't nervous, in fact we produced it ourselves, though the label credits Bill Perry. "Big Girl" was liked by all the local jocks, you know they'd always given a lot of spins to groups sounds—like that whole thing in the fifties started in Philadelphia. Yeah, I guess "Big Girl" was a bit like those old sounds. Soon it was the biggest record in Philly, that's when it was picked up for national release."

The Avco (formerly Avco Embassy) entertainment conglomerate had launched itself belatedly into the heady world of records and brought in two music world veterans—Hugo and Luigi—to run the Avco label. It was Avco who put "You're A Big Girl Now" out to a national audience. Its captivating sound of suggested innocence with Russell Thompkins soaring in a strange, vaguely nasal, falsetto with a ludicrous bass voice monologue made it a fair soul hit (No. 1 in New York). Avco who'd brought the group's contract as well as the disc's master, patted themselves on the back and looked around for a means to cement the Stylistic's success.

"When we were told Thom Bell would be producing us we were obviously pretty honoured. We knew about him of course. All his hits with Gamble and Huff and the Delfonics. Before we went into the studio with Thom he had worked hard on us . . . treated us like we were total newcomers to the music business. He made Russell sing a little bit lower and he worked with us so we'd sound right with the big orchestrations. When we did the actual session it only took six hours. He'd written a song with Linda Creed called "Stop Look And Listen". That's the one they put out first. It was a hit so quick even Avco were taken aback! When we heard the sound he was able to get with us we were really gassed. You know it's a shame a lot of things are hyped as being works of genius when they're not. So it sounds phoney when I say Thom is a genius. But he *is* man."

The recent Thom Bell feature in BM (issue

ROOST

two) documented how Thom, a classicly trained, unassuming man with a fine ear for counterbalancing the sound of the streets of R&B vocal groups with lush multi-instrument backings has brought the Stylistics truly phenomenal success. "You're My Everything" with an undulating, spaced intro and a sad little lyric guaranteed to dampen the eye of anyone who's loved and lost; or "Betcha By Golly Wow" pure teen-dream but with a quivering shimmering sound; or "People Make The World" a swirling piece of Whitfield-styled comment on the world's troubles; every track of "The Stylistics" album was used as a 45. It didn't of course end there.

"We recorded "Stylistics 2" in April '72. You know one of the things about Thom is that every track he puts down with us he works on like it's a potential single. So we got some big hits from that album too. "I'm Stone In Love With You", was a really big 45 for us of course. We came to Britain when that was out. Up until then your radio had ignored our records but that one they played . . . that one was a hit. We had a ball over in Britain, we loved working there and we knew sooner or later we'd be back for a new tour. It's taken a while of course but now it's happened we're all really excited at the thought of playing to some British audiences. You see recording is only one side of our activities, working on stage is also very important to us."

Although BM correspondent Dennis Hunt suffered from "falsetto overkill" when he saw the Stylistics in LA recently, the bulk of us will no doubt marvel at the super slick choreography and pin-point precise harmonies that the group have developed since becoming the darlings of the world's top night spots.

"Having "Rockin' Roll Baby" has helped our stage act, because that was the first big uptempo number for us. We've always included some fast songs in our stage act, we've used 'Backstabbers', 'Dance To The Music' but 'Rocking' is the one which was a smash for *us* . . . it really gets the kids movin' after they've stood and listened to our slow tunes. Yeah, that tune was different for us. In fact we laughed a little when Linda (Creed) first told us the story line . . . you know 'got a funky walk in his little orthopaedic shoes'. In many ways I think the things we do on 'Rockin' Roll Baby' album are our best things. A number called 'You Made Me Feel Brand New' is where I share the lead with Russell. That's the first time I come up front on one of our records.

"You know a funny thing about all our albums . . . people are still *listening* to them. Like a lot of records people listen to them when they're hits, but after a few months they stop playing them. I like to think our music is gonna last."

# War

*Papa Dee*

*Lee Oskar*

*Harold Brown*

**WAR have reached that critical stage in their career that calls for a necessary period of self-evaluation.**

Even though War has long outgrown their back-up band status suffered under the abrasive raspings of Eric Burden (the foremost negrophile in rock and roll), none of the others on the melodic front line—Charles Miller, Howard Scott and Lonnie Jordan who share between them reeds, guitars and keyboards—seems particularly eager to unleash their album chops in concert. Even though I have heard individual manifestations on different occasions, I have yet to see a concert in which all three come off with stellar performances.

Like many of the street funk or "progressive soul" bands, War relies heavily on rhythm for impact. Unlike many of those such as Kool and The Gang or The New Birth, whose models come from back-up bands like King Curtis and The Kingpins, The Markeys or Ike Turner's Kings of Rhythm (currently sporting the name, Family Vibes) and who have the ability to mix jazz influences with the Memphis sense of easy abandon that characterises most back-up bands; War's esoteric sense of formal construction in addition to a seeming lack of chops, combines to create a highly individual manifestation of the current trend, an individuality like that of Sly, and Earth, Wind and Fire. The problem with this style is that where Kool and The Gang and The New Birth, always have plenty of room for movement, War by the more narrow range of its reference, could become constricted. War is moody in intent at times drawing on texture as a relief from overdrive, interstellar or otherwise!

This is the point the group has reached. Their last album, "Deliver The Word", tended toward pomposity and the inflation of trivial ideas combined with self indulgence, provided an album that was saved only by some excellent editing on "Gypsy Man" and a version of "Me And Baby Brother" restyled in the successful mould of "The Cisco Kid". The rest of the album was almost uniformly a waste of precious vinyl and in having the wisdom to take a breather, War must recognise this.

War can be forgiven, however, because after at least two brilliant albums, and three innovative ones, the group has earned at least our tolerance, if not much more. Even though two of them were corrupted by Eric Burdon, the coming ability of the group was evident. And anyway, according to drummer and spokesman Harold Brown, it was all part of the master plan.

"It was all a plan, it was a plan from the beginning of time that everything would happen, and that was a plan in itself, down to that very last day, Armageddon!"

Brown says that the group started with

himself and guitarist Howard Scott when they were both about 13 or 14, placing their origin at least 13 years in the past. They were soon joined by B. B. Dickerson, Howard's cousin and eventually Charles Miller. Finally Lonnie Jordan talked his way into the group and The Creators were finalised. They soon found work in the Southern California, Compton-Long Beach area and by the time High School was out of the way they had made their decisions.

"We decided that we were gonna be musicians and this is what we really wanted to do, we just had it set in our minds that we would do it this way. We didn't want to go to college or to become lawyers or anything like that, we wanted to be musicians."

After being broken up by the armed services, marriages, divorces, the group decided to give it another try, this time as The Night Shift.

"We decided to get back together one more time and give it one more push. We decided if we didn't make it after this one more try we would look for it somewhere else, and then all of a sudden things started happening."

Among the people they ran into were football player Deacon Jones who introduced them to their manager Jerry Goldstien who introduced them to The Plan.

"Eric Burdon and Jerry and Steve Gold were running together at the time and they were trying to get something happening, but they were kinda disappointed because nothing was happening and Eric was just about ready to go back to Europe. We were both trying to get it going one more time and one night Lee Oskar came by with Jerry Goldstien when we were playing a club and he came up with his harmonica and we started jamming. At that time I didn't know Eric Burdon from anybody else and I thought Lee was Eric Burdon and I was very impressed. When I finally met Burdon the first thing he told me was 'Yeah, I got to have me two million dollars', and I was even more impressed. Eric didn't want to be with a group that he was the leader or anything, he wanted to be part of the group. Steve ran it down with us about how he would like us to work with Eric up to a certain point and then we would go off by ourselves, this was The Plan."

From out of that early collaboration came the hit "Spill The Wine" from the LP "Eric Burdon Declares War". That album and the subsequent "Black Man's Burdon" contains some of War's best material and should not be overlooked because of Burdon's presence. Songs like "Pretty Colors", "Gun", "Jimbo", all from "Black Man's Burdon" and most of the original material on "Burdon Declares War" are among War's best compositions.

Then as now, the group writes all their songs in collective jam sessions in which the best ideas are preserved and moulded into songs. Despite the cool reception given to "Black Man's Burdon" and "War", Brown has good reason to feel that "the plan has been going perfect". War is currently riding a gold streak that shows no signs of diminishing.

"Some people say we should have made it a year or two ago, but to me I think everything went the way it was supposed to. That tour we did with Isaac Hayes really did it. We were known in the rock circuit because of our association with Burdon, but the rhythm and blues circuit didn't know nothing about us. Most black people don't know that it was us and Burdon that did "Spill The Wine". But the plan has been going perfectly."

In two consecutive albums "All Day Music" and "The World Is A Ghetto", War created some of the most distinctive music the new genre has yet been responsible for. War's music is for the most part quite mellow, vocal or instrumental pyrotechnics are not part of the sound.

The group does not have a lead vocalist, a lead instrument or a lead songwriter, most of their work is a product of seven individuals working as one. Their jazz-funk orientation is evidenced by a song like "City, Country, City" a song that was covered by one of the leaders of the jazz-funk school, Lou Donaldson. The mellowness and sense of purpose that characterises their music, has a lot to do with their philosophies of themselves. Brown took this approach.

"We realise that we all need each other, we realise that we love each other and we realise that because we love each other, we have to give each other total freedom to exercise his ability and that way we complement each other. When we write a song, we all pitch in and share. We don't believe that there is no one man who writes a song because we all contribute. I *know* that this is the downfall of a lot of groups, because they get one guy who is the stronghold and wants to be the end, and everything centres on him and everything comes out sounding alike . . . But with us there is seven musicians and we share equally."

"Our music represents the signs of the times", Brown appears to be quite serious about this and even reaches into his pocket for proof. "I wrote a poem about that. It goes, 'Do you read your Bible to see what it says about the signs of the times? They are here today, murdering, lying, cheating, stealing; they are all a part of the signs of the times. Our music is influenced by these signs. Some people try to call it soul music, some try to call it rock, we get insulted when they call it rock.

"I guess you could call it progressive soul because the music progresses as our souls progress. But I trip on something else too, so I call it Street Jazz, because I pick up on all these rhythms from the street . . . Like I used to listen to The Last Poets, and I have never been to New York, but I knew what they were doing because it was all about the street, I knew what they were hearing in the street because I was hearing the same things. Five or six years ago we couldn't have made it because people weren't ready, they were just looking for polished Las Vegas acts. The way they put shows together it was like a newsreel, you would have just so much time and then off. I ain't cut out for that because you see, I grow too fast and my mind keeps moving constantly, if I wanted assembly line work, I would have stayed in a factory . . . People are more and more beginning to sit back and listen.

"They're finding out that they have feelings very much like someone who is performing. A lot of people trip on keeping their whole thing inside of them, they never talk to anybody about certain things, so they get to feeling that they are the only ones that get those kinds of pangs . . . I know that I get butterflies sometimes when I'm ready to go on stage and a lot of times I get to thinking that I'm less than a man because I get scared and I start to sweat. But then by looking some people in the face and saying 'Man I'm scared' and they'll say 'Yeah, I feel that way too'. So then I feel reassured because I realise that I *don't* have some rare disease, I ain't the only one that has them problems, and it makes me keep going . . . And that's what our music is all about, to try and break down these barriers."

**AROUND the time "Let's Stay Together" was becoming the biggest selling single of all time for London Records in the USA (beating the Stones' "Satisfaction"), the one-time leader of the Green Brothers gospel group made an astute observation about the irony of success: for one of a 1000 artists who yearly 'cross-over' from gospel music to soul.**

"When you first break away and you're not a star, y'understand, and you haven't gone out and boomed anybody in the pop field—you're still the same little mediocre town kid you always *were*. But *now* I can go wherever my gospel brothers are singing and I can just hop right up on stage and everybody will think that's great. But if I'd sung pop and failed—oh, I'd be a sinner, sinner, sinner."

Al Green is a star not a sinner and like most great soul artists has gained confidence to acknowledge, nay champion the cause, of the religious tradition whose culture he has plundered so skilfully in devising that iced, cool and gliding vocal style which has made him soul music's No. 1 with seven consecutive million-selling records.

"I still dig gospel music . . . the Swan Silverstones, the Mighty Clouds of Joy. The Soul Stirrers—Sam Cooke and Claude Jeter . . . fantastic, whew! Fantastic. All of my inspiration comes from above—I owe everything to gospel music."

Al was born on the April 13, 1946, in Forest City, Alabama and moved with his family to Grand Rapids, Michigan when he was nine years old. From the age of eight Al was singing that old-time religion with brothers William, Walter and Robert. But in 1964 Al risked the wrath of God . . . and his brothers . . . by forming a 'pop' group. The Creations, as they were called, were about as small time as they could be, even by Grand Rapids standards. Three years working tiny clubs like Battle Creek's El Grotto got Al nothing but threadbare suits and plenty of experience, and he became proficient in adapting his flexible tenor—with characteristic swoops of gospel style falsetto—for the popular soul songs of the sixties.

Some of the Creations split to play with Jr. Walker. In '67 the remaining ones, Curtis Rogers, Palmer James and Gene Mason called it a day as performers but Curtis and Palmer weren't through with music. They raised some cash and formed their very own, little ol' record company, right there in Grand Rapids. The label, Hot Line Music Journal, signed Al Greene (an 'e' was added) . . . and the Soul Mates. What exactly the Soul Mates did on the ensuing HLMJ sessions has never been adequately explained but they (Al's brother Robert and Lee Virgins) were credited on the label's first do-or-die release.

"One day Palmer James told me he'd written this *bad* song and he wanted me to sing it. But I wasn't interested. So he waited about nine months and asked me again. I said 'Well, O.K.' and we cut it and it was a hit. It sold 400,000. That was "Back Up Train".

The record was a revelation. It didn't—unlike most of that period's soul hits—indulge in tear-at-the-throat histrionic emotion. It was sweet soul . . . but with a hard core. A perfectly constructed bridge between 'group' singers' style and the grits of Daddy Otis. When Al soared to scatter fragments of falsetto the listener really felt it was a spontaneous gesture, not a contrived device. Local radio picked the record up and soon Larry Uttall and Bell Records were distributing Hot Line Music Journal's "Back Up Train" across the nation. As it became a national soul and pop hit the normal flurry of one-nighters and promises of super-stardom started. But alas this went wrong.

Al's follow-ups, "Lover's Hideaway" and

# Al Green

"Don't Hurt Me No More" were constructed similarly to Al's hit. Too similarly. The wistful and rather beautiful ballads didn't sell and the "Back Up Train" album missed out too, though oddly the 15-track bargain package of lilting ballads, including the great wailer "Guilty", was released in Britain. The accompaniments were subdued, occasionally inappropriate with cooing girls, but apart from a couple of up tempo tracks of startling mediocrity, there was a wealth of subtle, insinuating singing. Al was already singing songs like he was making love to them.

By '69 Al was back where he started—except now he was a solo soul singer working out on "Back Up Train" in small clubs and looking for a new record company and a new hit. One night he was doing a gig in Midland, Texas. In the audience was a trumpeter/producer who'd climbed on the Memphis train in the mid-sixties and was building a big reputation for himself and the London-distributed Hi label with a string of gritty, funky productions.

"I didn't know Willie Mitchell was there. During the show I started walking the tables: I got up on the tables singing to the people and they were applauding und screaming and singing along. Willie dug the show and wanted to bring me back to Memphis. First of all he asked me to come down and look around, and check out the studios, to see if I'd like it. It was cool and I liked it and I decided to try Hi Records. I was discussing things with Stax and Atlantic at the time but they had so many artists on their lists I thought I'd get lost. So I signed with Hi. Willie told me: "If you are really interested in becoming a *star* you've got to come and live in Memphis." So I did."

But Al's start with Hi began near-disastrously.

"A thing called 'One Woman' started me off with Hi. I recorded it before Isaac Hayes . . . see he'd come over to the studio where he heard my rendition of it and liked the song, which was written by Sandy Rhodes and Charles Chalmers. So Isaac went back over to Stax and put a version on his LP "Hot Buttered Soul"—the first song on the album."

To make matters worse, instead of releasing Al's superbly understated portrait of marital infidelity, they pushed him into the studio again this time with the song sheet for the Fab Four's "I Wanna Hold Your Hand" and released the outcome as Al's first Hi single. "To be honest I didn't like doing it and I still don't care too much for that particular song of the Beatles."

The attempt to make "Hand" into funk was successful in a fashion, but Al sounded as uncomfortable as he felt. When Hi did release "One Woman" that didn't sell much either. So if a funked up pop ditty didn't make it, nor an old-style soul ballad wailer, Hi decided to try him with a more "progressive soul" sound. "Right Now Right Now" had a bit of Sly, Hendrix and good hard funk and Al's vocal was harder and edgier than anything else he'd cut. It was a reasonable soul hit and the climb back had started. And the momentum was maintained.

"I was coming back from a date and Laura (Lee) and I both started singing the Temptations' thing 'I Can't Get Next To You'. And we agreed that it would be good to record it with a few alterations. So when I got to Memphis I suggested it to Willie and we cut it."

The "few alterations" were making a catchy, Detroit bubbler into a down-in-the-alley blues/funker. Willie's band of Mabon "Teenie" Hodges (guitar), Charles Hodges (organ), Leroy Hodges (bass) and Howard Grimes (drums) were able to produce a gut groove of steam hammer power, a groove which Al reacted to by a startling series of vocal acrobatics. The "Gets Next To You" album reinforced the mood, Memphis funk, Al Green style. His style was original, after all who else had that mesmerising range to use

Black Music Gallery

Al Green

Black Music Gallery

Ray Charles

over such solid accompaniments? All he needed was the right song to "break him pop".

"'Bout five o'clock one Friday morning, I was sittin' up on the side of my bed, 'cause I'm a bachelor you see, and I said to myself, 'I'm tired of being alone'."

If you don't believe "Tired Of Being Alone" is a classic you probably aren't reading Black Music. One of the great black music discs, a moving plea to a lost love, when he spirals into that "baaabeee" you can almost hear the tears splashing onto the mike. Al writes most of the lyrics, Willie Mitchell and M.G.s drummer Al Jackson handle most of the melodies. Once the formula as well as the sound had evolved there was no stopping them.

"After the first million seller "Tired of Being Alone" everyone said, "okay, one million seller, he won't do it again". So we had another, and another, and another, and . . . All the songs are a story. The story says I Can't Get Next To You and I'm Tired Of Being Alone so Let's Stay Together 'cos Look What You've Done To Me and you know I'm Still In Love With You so Call Me."

As far as sales go the figures are still pure storybook. But after the first couple of million sellers . . . in fact from the "I'm Still In Love With You" album, fans, critics and soul people have become increasingly worried . . . and worry might lead to irritation. Said Vince Aletti:

"The technique is brilliant—the incredible mobile vocals, carrying the songs in an intricate ebb and flow, and especially the rise of the falsetto, thinning out to almost nothing for the delivery of a particularly delicious line—but, ironically, as it's perfected it seems more obtrusive as a technique and less acceptable as an inspiration. The first flash of lightning is always the most exciting; after that they just brighten up the landscape. Such are the problems of professionalism. Each successive Hi album has intensified and polished Green's approach while it narrows his range of material. So the songs get better (or at least stay within a few points of "Tired Of Being Alone" and "Let's Stay Together" which

would be difficult to surpass) but they also get more and more the same."

Al: "There's so much on my head, it's a strain and I'm just one cat looking for all the answers. Willie comes to me and says we've got to have a new album, and as I write all the songs except maybe two, the material has to come out of my head. So right away I get to work. Sometimes I get behind because if I'm not writing a song I'm at the office working late, if I'm not at the office I'm at the studio recording, and if I'm not there I'm on the road doing gigs."

His gigs are, of course, a part of the legend. His two visits to Britain have been dazzling in the *star* quality he radiates while his voice seems as deftly acrobatic wailing into a mike at the Rainbow . . . or the Apollo . . . or the Copacabana as it does warbling his latest tender ballad on disc. Records and stage shows earn Al enough to live in splendid luxury in a 21-room house in its own 60 acres in elite Shelby Forest. And with Al living like a film star now he wants to be one.

"I'd like to see how well I can act, if I'm good at lying or not. I want to be sure all talents are explored. We turned down "Across 110th Street" and "Black Caesar". They wanted me to write the scores but I didn't feel it was right, all that killing, dope and girls. I'm trying to project love, happiness."

Recently, of course, there's been a 'Sam Cooke Story' movie rumour: "I'd like to go into films but I'm not really interested in doing the Sam Cooke film—they offered it to me but I said no . . . I think Sam was great but I want to be Al Green . . . not Sam Cooke . . . I want to keep my *own* identity.

"I've got a new album, just out in the States . . . I've written most of the songs though I do a version of "Unchained Melody". I think it's a fresh direction, a fresh approach. There's four or five possible singles on there. In a way it's a little different in overall sound from my last few things but it still has what I like to feel is the stamp of Willie and I . . . and that's the Memphis groove. I hope it will sell . . ."

# Bobby Bland

**"HE'S had more Hot 100 entries than the Beatles." That's the claim—a totally accurate one—in the Bobby Bland adverts scattered liberally throughout the U.S. trade papers.**

ABC/Dunhill records have captured one of black music's all time greats and they're determined that the greatness won't continue to be solely in the quality of Bland's music. No, they want greatness in his super-selling power, selling that is, to the millions of white kids eager to gobble up another blues-great packaged as skilfully as the new father-of-rock B. B. King. ABC will do it . . . they've got to. Bobby Bland should have been a rock super-star long before now.

"This Time I'm Gone For Good" is shaped up as a big single and "His California Album" has won more acclaim than a Kissinger peace treaty.

Robert Calvin 'Bobby' Bland was born in Rosemark, Tennessee on the 27th January 1930. But he was raised in Memphis. While a teenager he met the blues singer Rosco Gordon who gave encouragement to the big-built country boy with high cheek bones who hollered hymns at his Mom's church. Also coming on with tips about a future in music for Bobby was Billy 'Red' Love. And so by the late forties Bobby joined the Beal Streeters. They were a big local band. With an extraordinary all-star line-up which included Rosco Gordon, Johnny Ace and Earl Forrest, they were the hottest thing in black Memphis.

Soon, James Mattis, a well-known Memphis deejay, started recording the band. Gordon handled most of the vocals, with Ace and Bland doing odd songs, ranging down through home blues, boogie shouters and sweet ballads. Mettis' label, Duke Records was poorly distributed and it was when he sold Duke to

Don Robey, whose Peacock label was hot with The Original Five Blind Boys' "Our Father", that Johnny Ace and Bobby Bland became black household names.

B. B. King introduced Bobby to the Bihari Brothers, who were beginning to build their Modern/RPM record empire, and Sam Phillips, who was working as an independant for the Chess Brothers. Before Uncle Sam called in 1951, Bobby had cut a couple of discs. One side from the period "Drifting From Town To Town" (available once on several compilation albums) is a moaning blues of spiritual intensity.

"It started more or less like a church thing. This is my background, all the way up to the blues that I'm doing today. During that time, the Pilgrim Travellers was a very, very, hot group, we were like the local Pilgrim Travellers. We had five guys together and we never did anything professionally, like on records. But my sound started, it originated, from the church. My first record was in '51. We did it with the Bihari Brothers out of Los Angeles. My first session in the house of a friend of mine, Tuff Green. Ike Turner set up the date for me. He was playin' piano then, we used his guitarist which was M. T. Murphy", says Bobby.

The Beal Streeters broke up, Johnny Ace became possibly the first black superstar (before he blew his brains out playing Russian roulette) and Bobby went into the army.

"So I went in the service and I got out the last of May, May '54, '55 was the first time I did a nationwide thing recording—wise that was "It's My Life Baby"."

The disc was a national R&B hit alright and he and Duke bounded to bigger things. In 1957 Bland had a huge hit with "Further On Up The Road". Its ghetto sales were so great that it made the Hot 100 and stayed there for an unbelievable 21 weeks. He once told writer Charles Keil that his main musical influences were Ira Tucker (of the Dixie Humming-

birds), Roy Brown, Lowell Fulson and especially B. B. King.

"I really didn't get a style of my own until '57. I kinda patterned after four or five people really. '57 was the first time I had a style. I had been doing B. B. King for many years, I love the mellowness of his voice. I didn't find myself til 1957."

The people who helped him make the find were Wayne Bennett, a guitarist with fingers like quicksilver and a mellow-flowing style proving a perfect forte to underline the subtlety of Bobby's phrasing; Joe Fritz and Bill Harvey, whose bands backed Bobby in those early years of one-nighters and recording sessions; and Joe Scott. Joe was a fair trumpeter, a better writer, a fine arranger and occasionally a brilliant producer.

The fifties brought hit records and 250 shows a year. And the discs in the main were unbelievably good. In the early sixties they were better. There was "Cry Cry Cry" in 1960, Bobby croons the chorus so sweet and pure you'd think he studied with Sam Cooke and then bang! long drawn out cries of rabid exhortation. "I Pity The Fool" in 1961 with that scorching climax of "Look at the people, I know you're wondering what they're doing, They're just standing there, Watching you make a fool of me." Then in 1962 "Turn On Your Lovelight": pure gospel with tambourines, chanting choir and a head-thrown-back, hollering vocal. Popular R and B had, by '62, borrowed a lot of its inspiration from the church but seldom had the result recalled so vividly the gospel tradition.

The songs Bland performed were written by Joe Scott, Don Robey and Deadric Malone, the latter two rumoured to be one and the same—if you follow me. Sometimes the songs, or the arrangements jarred (the trite "Call On Me"—his second biggest 'pop' hit in 1963), but often his or Joe's choice of material was impeccable: the slyly ironical "Ain't Nothing You Can Do" or the T-Bone Walker

piece de resistance "Stormy Monday Blues". Through the sixties hits like "Ain't Doing Too Bad" (in '64), "Blind Man" (in '65) and "Rockin' In The Same Old Boat" (in '68) brought blues—kind of—into the charts.

Said Bland in '71: "I try to do blues in a ballad type way. Sometimes people classify you as a blues singer and nothing else. But I don't want this.

"So I do a variety of things. But what I have to rely on is the blues, because this is what I know, I grew up with this."

Gospel/soul/blues/ballads then, a form of honey-toned ballad singing which suddenly turns into raw, wailing storefront church music. He toured into the early sixties as half of the 'Blues Consolidated' package with Little Junior Parker.

When they finally split in '62 Bobby put his own extravaganza on the road: a whole revue with a warm up a big brassy band, Al "TNT" Braggs (and later Paulette Parker) and a girl group, the Bland Dolls.

Through the sixties and into the seventies his hits kept coming. "Good Time Charlie" or "Chain Of Love", he sang both with enough fire to burn holes in your speakers. On LP he was equally captivating. Although a few pop ditties like "Who Can I Turn To", and uneasy flirtations with Motownesque and wah-wah-funk didn't become him, but even when Andre Williams took over as producer from Joe Scott in the late sixties he still made persuasive, bluesy records.

But it's taken producer Steve Barri to bring out the best of Bland for a number of years. When ABC gobbled up Duke they wisely put Bland in a white rock framework but one which hasn't eroded his gospel blues roots. "This Time I'm Gone For Good" is perfect balance of the old blues style, today's sound, tomorrow's image building.

# Dandy Livingstone

**"I realised a long time ago that if you want to make it in this country you have to be commercial. It's all right selling ten, 12,000 or 15,000 to West Indians and have them say 'Yeah, that's a nice tune'. But that doesn't help me, I don't make anything out of selling 15,000 records. I wanna sell 250,000, 500,000, a million!"**

The West Indian music fans didn't stop and think "Oh this is too commercial" when they heard Dandy Livingstone's record 'Rudy A Message To You' in 1967 even though, on the surface, it was a novelty Rude Boy tune. They just bought the record and danced to the music. Yet even then the name 'Dandy' seemed to imply that his music could never be anything else but 'light-hearted'. Since that was what was expected, the underlying seriousness over the years of songs like 'Rudy A Message To You', 'Raining In My Heart', 'I'm Your Puppet' or 'Suzanne Beware Of The Devil' has been overlooked.

But now that Dandy Livingstone is purposely assigning a fundamental seriousness to his music, preconceived notions should be forgotten. Especially since Dandy's LP 'Conscious' is the result of some deep thinking on his part about the whole 'black' scene.

"I changed labels from Trojan to B&C Mooncrest because I wanted to change my musical direction and I believe that I wouldn't have been able to do that if I had stayed with Trojan. I just got to hate the way West Indians weren't getting anywhere. I've seen a couple of my fellow Jamaican artists make big hits and yet are no better off, so I wondered what's wrong y'know!

"I started recording the LP before I decided to change labels so they wanted me to scrap it but I said no I wanted it released. The

title 'Conscious' means that I'm aware of what's going on, the whole scene to do with black people, and I'm gonna keep on saying what's true. 'Black Connection' is in the same vein as 'Black Star', I'm still protesting! Connection means that black people must get together. 'I'm A Believer' and 'Glory Be Ay Glory Be You' are along the same lines, if you read the lyrics you'll see that they're all to do with the same thing."

Dandy Livingstone's real name is Robert Livingstone Thompson. He came to England in 1959 from Kingston Jamaica to join his parents when he was 15, and went to school, then to college to do an apprenticeship in engineering. The only other musician in Dandy's family is his cousin Ansell (of Dave and Ansell Collings) and his interest in singing didn't materialise until 1963.

"A friend of mine called Lloyd who's in Canada now, had a piano which he kept on banging day in, day out. I couldn't understand what he was playing, I don't think he knew either. Anyway we got together somehow, maybe three or four evenings a week. He would play and I would sing and it developed from there."

Dandy an Lloyd used to practise at a studio in the Cambridge Road, West London which is where he met Trojan boss Lee Gopthal who had a little shop upstairs at the time. In fact Dandy used to sell records for Lee on a part-time basis, either at school or in the evenings. One day Lee informed Dandy that someone was starting a label and they wanted two West Indian artists. So Mr. Thompson went along to an audition which resulted in his first ever record called 'What A Life' for the Carnival label in 1964.

"Carnival really wanted two guys for a duo but I couldn't find anyone else. So I just double tracked for the harmony and put it out

as Sugar and Dandy. Actually I and a guy called Roy Smith made a couple of records together later but he took off and another guy came and we called him Sugar Simone."

Radio Caroline's boss had connections with Dandy's label so the record was given a lot of plugs and it sold 25,000. Dandy realised then that singing was what he really wanted to do but soon afterwards the label folded and he had to cool it. He just kept on going to collegeworking to finish his toolmaking apprenticeship until he met Rita King in 1967. Back in '64 Rita King's Ska Beat label had surfaced from her premises in Stamford Hill, north London, and henceforth became the third-biggest label selling ska records in England after Melodisc and Island Records with releases by JA musicians such as Don Drummond, Baba Brooks, and The Wailers. One of the label's biggest hits was Dandy's 'Rudy A Message To You' in 1967.

"At that time the rude boy craze was going on in Jamaica, the guns and the bombs and things and I wrote the song from that inspiration. It sold about 30,000 and went into the top fifty. I had a good selling LP at the time as well called 'Rock Steady With Dandy'." Dandy left the Ska Beat label in 1968 to join Lee Gopthal at Trojan. First he made 'Move Your Mule' then 'Reggae In Your Jeggae', 'I'm Your Puppet' and 'Raining In My Heart' all of which sold very well. "Move Your Mule" comes from an old—time country saying in Jamaica I think. I'd say that about 80 per cent of my songs have been written after I got a title."

Ask any ex-Skinhead his ten favourite reggae records and 'Reggae In Your Jeggae' is always likely to be included.

"I made 'Reggae In Your Jeggae' in November 1968 and the Skinheads came about late in '69. But you know how these kids liked

to go back and look for early reggae things. That's what happened and they just liked this particular record, I didn't set out to make a 'skinhead' record."

The first person Dandy ever seriously produced was Audrey Hall. They made one album together (Dandy and Audrey), called 'I Need You' in 1968 after he had heard some of her demo tape.

The reggae version of 'Red Red Wine' by Tony Tribe which was a minor success was produced by Dandy Livingstone. He produced 'Suzanne Beware Of The Devil' for Nicky Thomas (before he himself had a hit with the song) but it didn't do anything. The Marvels' very good first LP—'The Marvels'—was also produced by Dandy and he's currently working on an album with Doris Troy.

'I'm Your Puppet' and 'Raining In My Heart', issued in 1970, were two of Dandy's best earlier tunes. The latter sold about 130,000 in fact but still didn't make the chart because the vast majority of the records were sold in 'specialist' shops which at the time did not supply sales figures for charts.

Between 1970 and '72 Dandy did very little. His only single releases were those I have mentioned and 'Take A Letter Maria' which only just missed the charts plus 'Won't You Come Home' and 'Morning Side Of The Mountain' which more or less bombed out. In fact he did nothing at all in 1971 and that was because he was doing some very serious thinking about his position in the music business.

"I wanted something to happen and it wouldn't happen, it hadn't been happening for me so I had a breather. I wrote some songs during that year and decided to go to Jamaica which I did in December. That's when I recorded 'Suzanne Beware Of The Devil' and 'Big City', in fact they were both done on the same session. It was worth it because I took the whole of '71 to re-vamp and re-direct myself. I came back to England and something happened."

Dandy recorded at Byron Lee's Dynamic Studio and an album containing 11 tracks—'Dandy Livingstone'—was released in 1972. Dandy's next single 'What Do You Want To Make Those Eyes At Me For' was taken from the LP but the DJs preferred the B side 'Suzanne Beware Of The Devil' which was not on the album.

"Well people talk about the devil makes you do this and the devil makes you do that. Well this guy had a little chick and it seemed to him that she was drifting away. He was just trying to tell her not to let the devil pull us apart y'know! Everybody said the song was 'different', I don't think so but maybe it's because I made it. It went to number 14 in the charts, which was good for me, it was what I'd been waiting for."

The follow up single 'Big City', went to number 27 in the charts and the next 'Come Back Liza' sold very well without making it. 'Black Star' is his best composition so far, it shows how accomplished he has become as a producer/arranger and it is proof that he has developed a much wider musical scope.

"I got really involved in 'Black Star'. I had the title then I said well as far as I am concerned I can't see any black stars in this country. When I sat down to write the song I realised that many black artists should be earning much more bread than they are at present. Even in America, where you've got big artists, black and white, the white artist still earns more! A black artist is just as good as a white artist if not better, right! So we shouldn't still be struggling to get an equal share."

# Billy Preston

**BILLY PRESTON'S appearance at the Bangladesh concert with Messrs. Harrison, Dylan, Starr, Clapton, and Russell, was one of the highlights in his long musical career. Billy was about the only non-"superstar" on the bill and even now he still does not consider himself one.**

"I'm no superstar I'm a superstar's musician! Bangladesh was a funky session, it was a real nice feeling and I enjoyed doing it 'cause George is my good friend. It was a worthy cause plus it did a lot for me. It was good exposure."

And although it was this occasion and his relationship with the Beatles that has had most to do with him being regarded as a star, the truth is that Billy has payed his dues and he attributes his success to his belief in God.

"When I worked with the Beatles I got a chance to see how they developed their songs from the start. It enlightened me, it didn't really effect the way I made music but I learned a lot of their techniques.

"God is the reason for my success, it's all been planned. I never go out and say I'm gonna do this or I'm gonna be the greatest or that I'm such a bad cat. I just believe that God works through me and guides me. I want to do right but there are so many bad things that you can get diverted by. You need a strong conviction. My material wealth does not contradict with my belief. God is almighty so that means God owns everything. God is not a poor God, you know what I mean!"

Billy Preston is a genuine soul artist. You cannot doubt that after seeing the amount of feeling and energy, that he gives to his music, and which reverberates between him, his band, and his audiences whenever he's out front on that stage.

Billy wants to spread the gospel to everybody. But many black soul fans don't regard him as a soul musician, since unlike James Brown or Curtis Mayfield he does not necessarily make music primarily for them.

"White people are hipper to me because of my association with the Beatles and for other reasons like those who come to my concerts are the ones who go by the Top Forty. But I do a lot of dates to mainly black audiences too. It doesn't worry me that more black people don't come to my concerts because eventually they will. It takes time. You can't draw everybody at the same time, you have to start somewhere you know!"

But black soul fans reckon that any black musician who plays regularly with white musicians and primarily to white audiences, has no interest in them, and so their reaction is 'the feeling is mutual!' And the trouble is that Billy's music—especially on his latest album "Everybody Likes Some Kind Of Music"—tends at times to be too diverse.

"Well you see, I was just trying to show that funky music is not the only thing I play. I mean you can do an album full of funk . . . you can always do that, but it's not a challenge, it doesn't fulfil your needs. So what I did on this album was show what I am capable of doing, and I can still make a funky album."

But won't black soul fans be further alienated by this musical direction?

"Yeah, well, they might be, but that's a narrow-minded way of thinking. If they want to they will be. But I'm reaching out for masses of people, I'm not reaching just for one race. Music is international. I wanna play for everybody.

"I don't want to be a James Brown or a Sly Stone or a Ray Charles. I don't want to be in that category, that's already been, man! They have their own audiences. What I want is a combination of all of the audiences, that's my goal. I'm not competing with them. That would be foolish.

"But I always do funky music if that's what you mean. I might do some reggae even! If that's what they wanna hear they can come and hear that but I'm gonna play something else as well. There are a lot of other people that I would like to come too. Unless somebody is bold enough to stand on their own and go someplace where nobody has ever been then we don't make much progress. I know that some black people might think that but that's not my reason for doing my thing and I hope that everybody eventually understands it."

Many Soul fans therefore have not heard anything by Billy outside of his hit singles: "I Wrote A Simple Song", "Otta Space", and "Will It Go Round In Circles". And they are missing a whole lot of good music. Things like "I'm So Tired", and "My Soul Is A Witness", or "God Loves You", and "Make The Devil Mad", from the LP "Music Is My Life".

"Well that's what I try to do, I try to do good. Anytime you try to do good there's always some bad things there, I just keep trying to do good and make the devil mad, I like that song too."

Billy Preston's appearance in the film 'St. Louis Blues' as the child W. C. Handy sealed his entry into show business at the age of ten. He got the part after being spotted by the film's producer while playing organ behind Mahalia Jackson on her travelling Gospel Show.

His next involvement with movies wasn't until when he wrote the title theme for the film 'Slaughter'. He had previously written the themes for 'The Bus Is Coming' and 'The Legend Of Nigger Charlie' but they were never used.

Between the acting and the composing is a period of about 14 years during which time Billy made eight albums. Three testify to the success that the A&M label has brought him (under the guidance of Robert Ellis his young enthusiastic manager) since leaving Apple.

His musical experience runs deep. It includes a tour with Sam Cooke and Little Richard at the age of 16, a regular TV spot on Shindig, a top Rock & Roll Show, a tour with Ray Charles and recordings on the Vee Jay label, his association with the Beatles and his Apple recordings, a tour with Lennon and the Plastic Ono Band, and sessions for many big

names like the Beatles, the Stones, Aretha Franklin and Sly Stone.

"Working with Sly was all right but it was very slow, slower than the Beatles record. He spent a lot of time on 'There's a Riot Going On' which took two years. We would play little bits and pieces, stop and then go back, we'd never finish 'em! But if you're really into it you can have a lot of freedom on his sessions. He picks the people who he likes playing with, who will inspire him to do what he wants to do, so it's a free for all!"

You have expressed a hope that you and other black musicians could get together on stage, is this a real possibility?

"Yeah that's something else that's never been done before with black stars, but white stars do it and it's profitable in many ways. It's gigantic, and they don't have to work the hardest! We can enhance our own thing, we can spread it better just by working together. We could do a tour, do an album, just draw more people and prove that we've got the power too. You can't knock success!

"Bobby Womack is game and Buddy Miles is interested, a lot of people are. I haven't talked to Stevie yet but I will and I read an interview where he was saying that he wanted to get out and play with other musicians too."

Who has had the most influence on you and your music over the years?

"Ray Charles, James Cleveland and Earl Grant. Ray Charles is the man, he is the genius, and you all don't know it! You talk about people stealing styles but he started singing the gospel type of songs and the Country and Western songs with a gospel flavour. Ray Charles is the man! If everybody don't know it they better get hip to it. He is the man! Earl Grant was a fantastic organ player, he was beautiful to watch he made some incredible sound on the Hammond Organ. James Cleveland was like the Ray Charles of Gospel. He has been like a father to me."

The God Squad is the name of the band which accompanied Billy on his recent European tour. They feature Manuel Kellough on drums with Kenny Lupper and Hubert J. Heard on keyboards.

"This group has been together for about three months now. I had a regular rhythm section before for about a year, which was a very good band but I wanted to do something different and I've always wanted to have a keyboard band. I've known this band for years, they feel the same way about music as I do and they play really well. It's like I was playing all the instruments at the same time but it sounds like 15 keyboards are on stage at the same time.

"I met Kenny Lupper when he was a little boy around ten years old 'cause he used to come to the church I used to play for with James Cleveland.

"Kenny used to watch me play and he could play one of my recordings exactly like me and it blew my mind.

"I met Hubie about six or seven years ago in Cincinnati, Ohio when I was on the road with Ray Charles. It was a Sunday morning and I went down into the neighbourhood looking for a church to go to. I met this old lady and we went to the one she was going to. When we got there this little boy ran over to me and said 'Are you Billy Preston?' And I said, 'No,' because I didn't want to play, y'know!

"The next thing I know this little boy goes out front to the organ and plays some of my old tunes like 'Billy's Bag' just like me and it was incredible, he's a fantastic musician.

"My drummer Manuel, I met him about five years ago. He's a great drummer, he was playing in a young band called The Rhythm Rebellion a very hip group of black cats. I didn't have a band then so I used them for a while. Eventually, when they started breaking up I just said 'hey man I wanna play with you!'

"So it was just me and Manuel at first and when I started getting dates I thought we'd better get a band together. We picked a band—young guys—a good band but sometimes you can get hung up with egos and get carried away by a lot of things, so you have to be careful especially about being black. Groups break up because of these problems many times.

"In the end I got this present group together and it's very good, all the fellows are really nice, good musicians and we're on the same trip."